FREEDOM

FREEDOM

The True Perspective About *Women* In Ministry

SECOND EDITION

Clement C. Butler

FREEDOM
The True Perspective about Women in Ministry

Copyright © 2021 Clement C. Butler. All rights reserved. Except for brief quotations in critical publications or reviews, no part of this book may be reproduced in any manner without prior written permission from the publisher. Write: Permissions, Wipf and Stock Publishers, 199 W. 8th Ave., Suite 3, Eugene, OR 97401.

Resource Publications
An Imprint of Wipf and Stock Publishers
199 W. 8th Ave., Suite 3
Eugene, OR 97401

www.wipfandstock.com
PAPERBACK ISBN: 978-1-6667-1760-0
HARDCOVER ISBN: 978-1-6667-1761-7
EBOOK ISBN: 978-1-6667-1762-4

Unless otherwise indicated, Scripture references are taken from the King James

Version of the Bible. Please send comments and questions to

approvedworkmanministries@yahoo.com

Please visit our website: www.approvedworkmanministries.com

Follow us on Twitter @242teacher

CONTENDERS FOR THE FAITH

CONTENTS

Acknowledgements vii
Foreword ix
Introduction xiii

1. Changing the Perspective: Unity and Equality 1
   A Particular Lens 1
   Male-Oriented Bible? 2
   God's Original Design for Humanity 5
   Help Meet 9
   The Impact of Sin and Restoration 12

2. Context Provides Perspective 16
   The Purpose of the Book 16
   The Message of Unity and Equality 17
   The Context and Perspective of Scripture 20

3. The Context and Perspective of 1 Corinthians 26
   Women Speaking in the Church 26
   Reconciliation of 1 Corinthians 14:34-35 29
   The Context of the Book of 1 Corinthians 30

    The Report from Chloe's Household and Other Reports 32
    Responses to the Letter Received From the Corinthian Church 34

4. Covering for Women 49
    Wearing Hats 49
    Prophecy and Prophesying 53
    Prophecy and Prophesying Defined 53
    Reconciling Scripture Regarding Head Covering 56
    Hierarchy of Authority: Covering from God's Perspective............................ 58
    Weaker Vessel 62
    Ministry Covering for Women 67
    The Progressive Nature of the New Testament 70
    The Qualifications for Office 76
    Ministry Gifts 81

5. Women Teaching and Usurping Authority Over the Man 83
    The Context of Ephesians and 1 Timothy 83
    Let the Woman Learn in Silence 88
    Teaching and Usurping Authority Over the Man 90
    God's Original Order 93

6. One In Christ 99
    Gender Identity in Christ 99
    Clothed in Christ 100
    Notable Women in Scripture 104

Conclusion 113
References 115

ACKNOWLEDGEMENTS

This book is dedicated to the memory of my mother, Ida Mae Winters who was one of the strongest women I have ever known. Unquestionably, her sacrifices created a path that allowed me to flourish in life. Her strength continues to live on, especially in my sisters, Rochelle and Karen.

Special thanks to Dr. Mary Banks and Dr. Betty Cleare, wise master builders who laid a great foundation for the work the Lord had purposed for me. Special thanks also to Angela Palacious, whose pioneering spirit coupled with her graciousness continues to be an inspiration to everyone.

FOREWORD

Matters concerning women in ministry have been some of the most rising and relevant topics of all time. In fact, controversial debates on these subjects have escalated more than ever in the 21st Century as women discover their identities and purposes in Jesus Christ. Consequently, many of them are realizing they are called to be more than Sunday school teachers, choir directors, ushers, women auxiliary leaders, and prayer band warriors.

Admittedly, God has given household orders to which women are subjected. However, I believe in ministry, God can use any vessel that is submitted to Him.

> It shall come to pass in the last days, says God, I will pour out my spirit upon all flesh. Your sons and daughters shall prophesy, your young men shall see visions and your old men shall dream dreams. (Acts 2:17)

Women around the world have been struggling with their spiritual identities and positions in the kingdom for decades. This is primarily so because of spiritual leaders who have confined them based on their interpretations of the writings of the apostle Paul. These leaders have misconstrued the apostle's teachings about the role of women and their positions in the church. As a consequence, women have been packaged in boxes too small for their destinies.

Thankfully, as a submitted female millennial minister of the gospel, I am fortunate enough to have a liberated spiritual leader who saw the call of God upon my life, nurtured it over the years, affirmed it, and released me to fully operate in it.

Many women around the world are brimming with untapped potential. They have prophetic, deliverance, and apostolic gifts locked inside of them just as some of the great women in the Bible. However, today, many women are dying within because of ostracism, spiritual manipulation, discrimination, stagnation, and disapproval from spiritual leaders.

I firmly believe that leaders who do not have faith in or support women in ministry do their organizations a disservice. They hinder a generation that can be greatly impacted as a result.

Freedom: The True Perspective about Women in Ministry by Clement C. Butler is an erudite, thorough, and revelatory work. It unfolds the biblical truths about women in ministry that have been gravely misunderstood in Christendom.

This exceptional work gets to the heart of the matter and is one of the most profound, in-depth, and insightful reads; it brings clarity to curious minds.

If you want to achieve a spiritual understanding of the Word of God as it relates to women in the Bible and women today, this book is indispensable.

Undoubtedly, I highly recommend this masterful work and believe it will be the key to filling the gap between women who are really called to ministry and the leaders who are apprehensive about women in ministry.

The revelation and wisdom in this book will open your eyes to the possibility of women becoming all that they can be in God and in the kingdom. It is a must-have for every generation.

Read each page with an open mind and peel the wisdom from every paragraph. Embrace the practical principles and be free!

I commend this work to you without reservation.

Tanya R. Duncombe
CEO and Founder
TRD Ministries

INTRODUCTION

Over the years, I have had numerous conversations with both men and women regarding the veracity of women in ministry. Admittedly, as it pertains to church doctrine and practice, this matter remains a highly debated topic. In fact, many people hold opposing views concerning it. Obviously, some support it, while others are adamant that women should not be in ministry. Interestingly, the persuasion that women should not be ministers is not limited simply to men. Some women also share that conviction. Moreover, entire denominations, based on their interpretation of Scripture, remain polarized concerning women ministers and are often identified by these limitations.

On one occasion, a young man who is opposed to women in the ministry said he took that stance because of the structure of his denomination and their teachings. Nevertheless, denominational doctrines or traditions of men are not replacements for the truth of the Scripture. Furthermore, any teaching that is not supported by Scripture has to be reexamined and abandoned.

As a student of the Word of God, I have an appreciation that the Bible is the final authority on every subject matter. Therefore, individual thoughts, traditions of men, feelings, and personal preferences do not outweigh the conclusion of Scripture. In this respect, the Bible should truly be regarded as the constitution and held above every other opinion.

In the Bahamas, the spirit of the Constitution says that when any other law is not consistent with the Constitution, the Constitution shall prevail and the other law shall, to the extent of the inconsistency, be void. Hence, any doctrine or teaching that is inconsistent with Scripture (the Constitution) should be discarded. Furthermore, in using this analogy, for the truth of the Scripture to prevail, it has to also be rightly divided (2 Timothy 2:15). *As a principle, truth always brings liberty with it and is not intended to create bondages and limitations.* Jesus said in John 8:32, "And you shall know the truth, and the truth shall make you free." Truth, therefore, liberates us from conditions of confinement. The result is freedom; hence, the title of this book.

During my tenure in ministry, I have met many strong, anointed women who are unquestionably called by God as leaders in the body of Christ. However, their impact is somewhat discounted as there are those who because of gender bias, dismiss or question their influence. Furthermore, many women are persuaded that they are called by God to function in ministry. Yet, some cannot thoroughly validate their positions through Scripture. To this point, I say, "If you believe it, be prepared to defend it." For what is the point of having a conviction without the ability to offer a persuasive scriptural explanation to support it?

Over the next several chapters, a comprehensive examination will be conducted regarding the sureness of women in ministry. Undoubtedly, at the conclusion of this book, not only will the chains of religion and tradition be removed, but also, in its place, a concrete defense will be provided against those who are otherwise persuaded.

Any organization or house that intentionally diminishes the abilities of its members can never come to its full potential and purpose. In this hour of awakening, the time is now that all members of the household of faith become fully engaged in the work that the Lord has called us to. This obviously includes both men and women labouring together with God.

CHANGING THE PERSPECTIVE: UNITY AND EQUALITY

A Particular Lens

A few months ago, I went for an eye exam. The main purpose was to conduct a visual acuity test in order to assess my vision. Even though I had recently turned forty-five, it was more of a routine visit than anything else. As was done on previous occasions, the optometrist used the phoropter to test my eyesight and to determine whether or not I required glasses. You know the drill. While looking through the device, the eye doctor flips different lenses in front of your eyes to measure your ability to see varying details of different sizes. At the same time, the optometrist asks the question, "Which is better, A or B?" and depending on your response, he/she can make an assessment. After the examination, it was determined that I needed glasses for reading. However, the truth is that even though I got them, I never use them.

A good portion of the doctrine pertaining to the role of men and women in the church is a result of examining the Scriptures through the lens of male dominance. As a result, we have a culture in the church of gender suppression, which has also overflowed its banks into society in general. For it is reasonable to think that if someone is against women in a leadership role in the church, this disposition may also be prevalent at work or in other interactions with women in leadership. We seem to be engaged in a contentious struggle, reenacting the battle of the sexes in every facet of our lives. What was once a phrase used to describe a tennis match now seems to be played out in the church, the workplace, and even in the family.

If there is one thing history has taught us, it is that one group's oppression against another often results in rebellion. The revolution that has spurred the feminist movement is partly a revolt against those who have abused truth. As the body of Christ, we have certainly done ourselves a disservice by viewing Scripture through myopic lenses in relation to women.

Male-Oriented Bible?

At face value, it would appear that the Bible is a male-oriented book. In fact, the language used would seem to suggest that. For instance, as it pertains to ministry, most of the pronouns in Scripture are masculine in nature such as he, him, or his. Additionally, the word "brethren" is constantly used in Scripture in reference to all believers. The following scriptures highlight this example.

> For whom he did foreknow, he also did predestinate to be conformed to the image of his Son, that he might be the firstborn among many brethren. (Romans 8:29)

> Now concerning spiritual gifts, brethren, I would not have you ignorant. (1 Corinthians 12:1)

> To the saints and faithful brethren in Christ which are at Colosse: Grace be unto you, and peace, from God our Father and the Lord Jesus Christ. (Colossians 1:2)

> Having therefore, brethren, boldness to enter into the holiest by the blood of Jesus. (Hebrews 10:19)

In addition to the word brethren, the Bible also uses the term "sons of God" to refer to all believers. For example:

> But as many as received him, to them gave he power to become the sons of God, even to them that believe on his name. (John 1:12)

> For as many as are led by the Spirit of God, they are the sons of God. (Romans 8:14)

> Behold, what manner of love the Father hath bestowed upon us, that we should be called the sons of God. (1 John 3:1)

Indeed, for a woman, the usage of these words could be somewhat disconcerting. However, to have the proper perspective on the Scriptures, there are several salient factors to consider while reading or studying the Bible.

First, the writings were subjected to a particular cultural environment, which, for the most part, was a patriarchal society. Specifically, in the Old Testament, the societies were primarily male-dominated. This dominance encompassed every aspect of life including family, religion, and government. It was in this dominant cultural environment that the Scriptures were written. However, despite this premise, in some cases, the language is not gender-specific and includes both male and female. In the first instance, the word "brethren" in the New Testament is the Greek word *adelphos*. One of its definitions refers to belonging to the same people or family. Hence, it is a generic term to depict all those who belong to the family of God irrespective of gender. Additionally, the reference to believers as sons of God is also a legal designation as sons are the ones who receive the inheritance determined by the Father. Furthermore, in terms of purpose, a son serves as the Father's representative to fulfill His purpose. Therefore, the word "son," which includes both men and women, is an all-inclusive word because of what a son represents to the Father. Similarly, in reference to representative terms used in Scripture, the Bible uses the analogy of a husband and wife to illustrate the relationship between Christ and the church

(Ephesians 5:21-33). In this example, it compares the church to a wife and describes Christ as her husband. Therefore, the comparison is used to signify Christ's relationship with all believers, both men, and women. In this instance, the word "wife" as we saw with the word "son" is not gender-specific. Rather, the emphasis is on what a wife represents.

Therefore, in nominal terms, the Bible may have the appearance of a male-oriented book, but it certainly is not. Based on the Father's purpose for humanity and His kingdom objective, it is fundamentally a book that promotes unity and equality.

God's Original Design for Humanity

Now that we have addressed the notion of a male-oriented Bible, there is another factor to consider in relation to men and women. It is the subject of God's original design for humanity. This inclusion will strengthen the premise of unity and equality as it pertains to males and females. In fact, once we have determined this fundamental truth, then every other opinion on the subject becomes less important. In my writings, I often conclude that the seed of all Scripture is found in the book of Genesis. Therefore, it is impossible to understand the Bible without an understanding of the context of "the book of beginnings." In that regard, what is the Bible's account of the creation of man and woman from God's perspective?

> 26. And God said, Let us make man in our image, after our likeness: and let them have dominion over the fish of the sea, and over the

fowl of the air, and over the cattle, and over all the earth, and over every creeping thing that creepeth upon the earth.

27. So God created man in his own image, in the image of God created he him; male and female created he them. (Genesis 1:26-27)

According to Scripture, both male and female were created in the image and likeness of God. This in itself is a statement of unity and equality, for both men and women bear God's image and likeness. Furthermore, in Genesis 1:26, the word "man" derived from the Hebrew word, *Adam*, is a generic term that denotes all humanity including male and female. Hence, God used the term, "man" to describe the entire human race. The term embraces man and "womb-man." This position is also supported in Genesis 5:1-2:

1. This is the book of the generations of Adam. In the day that God created man, in the likeness of God made he him;
2. Male and female created he them; and blessed them, and called their name Adam, in the day when they were created.

God created man in His image and His likeness so that humanity (male and female) would serve as His representatives on Earth and function like Him. It was only fitting that those who were ordained to represent Him look like Him and have the capacity to function like Him. Therefore, the fact that women were made in the image and likeness of God means that from the beginning, God had predetermined they would also represent Him and function on His behalf.

Specifically, what does it mean to be made in the image and likeness of God? John 4:24 says that God is a Spirit. This signifies His very substance or nature. Therefore, when He created humanity, He made us like Him in that we are also spirit beings. Genesis 2:7 says that the Lord breathed into man the breath of life and man became a living soul. This means God deposited His essence or life into the earthly body that He formed. Along these lines, Job 32:8 says, "But there is a spirit in man: and the inspiration of the Almighty giveth them understanding." Hence, inside every human body, there is a human spirit that is eternal in nature.

Furthermore, He also created us in His image, which pertains to our human shape or form. The physical body or temporary house that we are in is not the true essence of who we are. As spirit beings, we need our earthy bodies to function on the earth. Although spirits are not identified by gender, ethnicity, or social status, we seem to place more emphasis on the earthy house than the real person in the house. For more on this please see my book, *What Happens When You Die?*

Additionally, Genesis 1:26 also says that both males and females were given dominion over the earth or ordained to rule. Therefore, based on Scripture, we can conclude God determined from the beginning that both male and female were created to have dominion or to rule. This too is a pronouncement of unity and equality.

At its core, the Bible is simply a book about a King establishing His kingdom. To understand the communication of Scripture, particularly in relation to men and women, it is essential to embrace the perspective of a kingdom concept. To validate its kingdom position, you will find that the Scripture is filled with words such as king, queen, throne, dominion, majesty, royal, reign, scepter, etc., which are all affiliated with kingdom rule. Hence, it is of no coincidence that right after creating man, the Lord uses the word, "dominion," which has kingdom significance. The word dominion means:

- Control or the exercise of control
- The power to govern
- Sovereignty
- A territory or sphere of influence or control; a realm
- The territory subject to the control of a government

Based on the definitions of dominion, man (male and female) was given governing influence or control over the earth. In essence, God set up His kingdom/government on Earth and placed humanity here as His representatives, made in His image and likeness. Therefore, He was extending His kingdom dominion on Earth through those who bore His image and likeness. Indeed, this paragraph has a wealth of insights, but for more on that, please refer to my books on *God's Eternal Purpose Volumes 1 and 2*.

When God created humanity, He did so in a kingdom environment where both male and female were called "man." Hence, in God's kingdom environment, there is no distinction between male and female. In addition to kingdom conditions, a family setting also existed in the beginning chapters of Genesis. This is where the order of creation mentioned in 1 Timothy 2:13 applies. It says, "For Adam was first formed, then Eve."

Help Meet

In establishing a good foundation for this discussion, we need to have the correct perspective regarding the term "help meet." Additionally, this understanding will also provide an appreciation for the dynamics that exist in a husband and wife relationship. As it pertains to the creation of the woman in Genesis Chapter 2, the expression "help meet" is often discussed with varying conclusions. Among the predominant opinions, it is used to suggest that the woman was created in a subordinate position compared to that of the man. However, all doctrine must be based on the true perspective of Scripture and not on denominational convictions or personal feelings. For this to occur, the Bible should be allowed to interpret itself in consideration of God's original purpose in the creation of the woman. In that vein, let's first consider the reason God made the woman.

Genesis 2:18 says, "And the LORD God said, It is not good that the man should be alone; I will make him an help meet for him." In principle, the passage says that the woman was created so that the man would not be alone. Based on Genesis 2:20, all the other living creatures had help meets. However, Adam was the only one of his kind. In other words, he was the only human being on earth. According to the *Free Dictionary* by Farlex and in harmony with the scriptural context, one definition of the word "alone" is to be unique or without equal. All the other living creatures had equals. However, in terms of his species, Adam was unique. Therefore, the woman was created so that the man would not be the only one of his kind. She was created so that he would not be without an equal.

Of note, the passage does not say that the woman was created because the man was "lonely." The word "lonely" is a condition of being unhappy, which could be a consequence of being alone or without companionship. Therefore, being alone is a state whereas being lonely can be a resulting condition. Hence, the primary reason God created the woman was that the man was the only one of his kind or species. Notice that even in this pronouncement from God, there is no implication of the woman being created inferior to the man. It was simply to address the matter of him being alone.

In addressing his state of being alone, the Lord used the specific term "help meet" in reference to the purpose of the woman. Therefore, let us define "help meet." The term "help meet" is the Hebrew word *ezer* and it means the following:

- The opposite part or counterpart
- A mate
- One who helps or a helper
- To surround (protect or aid)
- Succorer or deliverer

What is interesting is that the same word *ezer* is used throughout the Old Testament and often refers to the Lord as man's help or helper. Let's look at a few of the Scripture verses:

> And the name of the other was Eliezer; for the God of my father, said he, was mine help, and delivered me from the sword of Pharaoh. (Exodus 18:4)

There is none like unto the God of Jeshurun, who rideth upon the heaven in thy help, and in his excellency on the sky. (Deuteronomy 33:26)

But I am poor and needy: make haste unto me, O God: thou art my help and my deliverer; O LORD, make no tarrying. (Psalm 70:5)

1. I will lift up mine eyes unto the hills, from whence cometh my help.
2. My help cometh from the LORD, which made heaven and earth. (Psalm 121:1-2)

Happy is he that hath the God of Jacob for his help, whose hope is in the LORD his God. (Psalm 146:5)

In the English language, the word "helper" is often considered to be someone who is subordinate to another or someone under a person in authority. Hence, when it comes to the perspective of a wife or a woman, this is the common implication. However, based on the context of Scripture and its usage in the Hebrew language, *ezer* refers to someone who has the power or ability to provide help. It speaks of someone who has the strength to help. Therefore, the Bible refers to God as our *ezer*, for He has the power to do so. With the word being used to describe God Himself, this eliminates the concept of "help meet" as a pejorative position.

The usage of the word *ezer* in the creation of the woman provides the foundation for God's original intent for both man and woman and serves as the bedrock of their relationship. Genesis 2:18 says that man had no counterpart or that he was alone. Therefore, the Lord created a "suitable helper" for him. Again, based on the context of the word *ezer,* it does not imply someone who is less than, for it is also used of the Lord as He is our helper. In fact, the perspective of "help meet" has nothing to do with one's position but rather of one's function. Along those lines, a help meet can be someone in authority, an equal, or a subordinate. Therefore, when the Lord created woman, He created her to function as a counterpart with the power and ability to help man. Unlike the rest of creation, the man had no one to surround or aid him. He didn't have a mate or someone to help him.

The Impact of Sin and Restoration

Genesis 2:16-17 says,

16. And the Lord God commanded the man, saying, Of every tree of the garden thou mayest freely eat:
17. But of the tree of the knowledge of good and evil, thou shalt not eat of it: for in the day that thou eatest thereof thou shalt surely die.

As a result of sin, certain conditions changed relative to the relationship between God and humanity, as well as between a husband and his wife. Based on the disobedience mentioned in Genesis 3:6-7, the penalty for sin involved spiritual death and personal or individual judgments for the man and woman. First, due to transgression, humanity, in accordance with the judgment of Genesis 2:17, experienced spiritual death. In simple terms, spiritual death means separation from God. Hence, humanity became estranged from both the kingdom of God and the family of God. Additionally, God's kingdom influence on Earth was interrupted and another kingdom dominion was introduced. That other dominion was the kingdom of darkness (Colossians 1:13). Therefore, the kingdom environment in which male and female were equal ended. Consequently, through sin, humanity lost its dominion and became representatives or citizens of another kingdom. This was the kingdom consequence as a result of sin, which impacted all humanity.

Additionally, there were personal judgments, which were specific for the man and the woman, particularly a husband and his wife. In relation to the woman (wife), Genesis 3:16 says, "And thy desire shall be to thy husband, and he shall rule over thee." With the reference to husband, this speaks specifically to a family setting. Hence, in a family environment, the husband became the head of his wife and serves as her covering (1 Corinthians 11:3). Additionally, until the kingdom of God had been reintroduced on Earth, *this principle of male dominion governed all relationships and activities between men and women, whether married or unmarried.*

When Jesus came and said in Matthew 4:17, "Repent: for the kingdom of heaven is at hand," this represented the reintroduction of the kingdom of God on Earth and its principles. This provided the opportunity for humanity to be reunited with the kingdom of God and the family of God. Therefore, the Father's original order from the beginning regarding the kingdom's position and function for males and females was reestablished. Just as it was in the beginning, based on God's original design, in a kingdom environment there is no distinction between male and female. Hence, as it pertains to the church, which is the representation of the kingdom of God on Earth, male and female categories do not exist. Nevertheless, because of sin and the ensuing judgment, as it relates to a husband and wife relationship, there is still a distinction: the husband is the head of the wife.

God left this structure in place to provide order to the family and to serve as a witness of the relationship between Christ and the church, which is also a family (Ephesians 2:19, 1 Peter 2:10). God left Himself a witness in creation of how a family, including His, should function. The family represents a natural example of the relationship between Christ and the church. For this reason, Ephesians 5:23 says, "For the husband is the head of the wife, even as Christ is the head of the church." This is not a model of suppression where one is inferior but simply a pattern of responsibility and function. Unfortunately, the church has confused the family setting with the kingdom environment thereby creating restrictions for women in contradiction of the Scripture.

Furthermore, notice that the individual judgments for the man and woman occur after the Lord foretells His redemptive work in Genesis 3:15. Therefore, the work of redemption pertains specifically to sin and humanity's restoration of the kingdom of God. Hebrews 9:11-15 classifies it as eternal redemption and eternal inheritance. However, this is unrelated to the personal judgments of Genesis Chapter 3. First, as mentioned, the man became the head or the covering for his wife.

In a family setting, the husband has been given the position of authority in relation to his wife. In addition, the sentence for the woman also included pain during childbirth (Genesis 3:16). Moreover, as it pertained to the man, the conditions under which he would work became difficult. Work itself was not the judgment, for man worked prior to this pronouncement (Genesis 2:15). However, after sin, the ground was cursed, and the conditions of work became strenuous (Genesis 3:17-19). The Lord said, "In the sweat of thy face thou shalt eat bread." Despite the redemptive work of Christ, none of these conditions have changed.

Now that a good foundation has been established concerning God's original design for man and woman and the distinction between what applies to a kingdom environment, as well as what pertains to a marriage or family setting has been made, we can progress in our discussion regarding women in ministry.

The reason for so much confusion regarding this subject is a lack of understanding of what applies to the kingdom of God and the church, as well as what is relevant to a family atmosphere.

CONTEXT PROVIDES PERSPECTIVE

The Purpose of the Book

In many churches today, most congregations comprise of women. Their presence is visible and indelible, from the pulpit to areas of hospitality and everything in between. This influence is true, not only regarding the church but also in relation to schools, the workplace, and many other institutions. Hence, we can neither ignore the impact of women in society as a whole nor minimize the role they continue to play in many areas of everyday life. Without question, women have made tremendous contributions, particularly in ministry. I am certainly the beneficiary of such stewardship.

Let me be clear, the basis of this book is not hinged on this premise, and it is not to promote a feminist agenda. Furthermore, the perspectives of this book are not based on "evolving to twenty-first century standards" concerning women. On the contrary, its specific purpose is to provide scriptural clarity and liberty as it relates to women in ministry. In that vein, this volume intends to address the subject from God's perspective. Particularly, discussing references that are erroneously used to promote inequality between men and women in the church. Additionally, this book is not specific to women only. It is also designed for men as misunderstandings create limitations for everyone. So true is the popular saying by John F. Kennedy, "A rising tide lifts all boats."

The Message of Unity and Equality

In Matthew 12:22-26, while answering the Pharisees concerning healing, Jesus gave a principle that a house divided against itself cannot stand. In 1858, Abraham Lincoln, who became the sixteenth president of the United States of America, echoed the same sentiments while speaking against slavery in his speech "A Divided House." In consolidating the two references, the reasoning is that any house that operates with fractions and contends with itself cannot endure. On the other hand, the reverse is also true, which is that a unified house is a formidable force.

We live in a world where the concept of equality, particularly between men and women, is the nucleus of many discussions. However, the message of equality also has to be the message of unity, for you cannot have one without the other or one at the expense of the other. Without unity, equality is imbalanced. If the struggle for equality has a diminishing effect on the other party, the result will still be inequality, just in the other direction.

One of the tenets of the gospel of Christ is the message of unity and equality, as well as the elimination of things that divide us. Unequivocally, the gospel does not promote the concept of division. For example, Ephesians Chapter 2, with respect to the Jews and Gentiles, speaks of removing the walls that created divisions. It promotes fostering the unity of a single household (Ephesians 2:11-22). However, the misinterpretation of Scripture has created fractions in the household of faith. Moreover, it has also been the fuel for denominational expansion, which has contributed to the discord between men and women.

Oftentimes, when the conversation of women in spiritual leadership roles is tabled, the general defense by many proponents include prominent women in Scripture. This consists of women such as Deborah and Esther in the Old Testament or Mary and Priscilla in the New Testament. The emphasis of their position is primarily on the significance of the responsibilities they undertook despite their gender. While this is indeed a noteworthy approach, difficulty is usually encountered when certain New Testament scriptures are brought into the equation or when the overall concept of the Law is factored in. Except for Galatians 3:28, which points out that, in Christ, there is neither male nor female, there are other scriptures that are seemingly more difficult to navigate around when to comes to women in ministry. Specifically, these are 1 Corinthians 14:34-35, 2 Timothy 2:9-14 and for good measure, 1 Corinthians 11:3-16.

Without question, the achievements of some of these

noteworthy women will be acknowledged in this book. However, I am certain that there will be a greater appreciation for truth once we have reconciled all scriptures on this important subject. In addition to Galatians 3:28, the fulfillment of Joel's prophecy in Acts 2:1-13, which speaks of both sons and daughters prophesying, is also used with great regularity. While this too is valuable relative to this discussion, expansion on this will also be postponed until Chapter 4. Therefore, the question is how do we take the conclusions of the first chapter and reconcile them with New Testament teachings on women in ministry?

While conducting a seminar on rightly dividing the Word of God a few years ago, I used 1 Corinthians 14:34-35 as the basis of the discussion. At face value, this passage appears to suggest that women are to remain silent in the church. In fact, it seems to insinuate that they are not permitted to speak at all. Without explaining the passage or stating my position on the scripture, I observed as the attendees were torn on the true context of the passage, and they appeared somewhat perplexed. During this time, I could hear comments by several women in the room: "I know God called me," but no reconciliation of the passage was offered. As mentioned, what is the point of believing something if you are unable to validate it in Scripture? However, much to their delight, after offering a detailed analysis of the scripture, there was a sigh of relief as if a burden had been lifted.

Again, I reiterate that the objective of the new covenant is to bring about liberty or freedom. Therefore, this passage, along with the others used in opposition to women ministers will be covered in detail throughout the course of this book to substantiate this position of liberty. What better way to engage the detractors of women in ministry than to use the very arrows they themselves shoot?

The Context and Perspective of Scripture

Before plunging into the discussion, I wish to establish a foundation relevant to scriptural interpretation. For something that has produced invisible chains in the household of faith for centuries, the keys of freedom require a systematic approach. Therefore, patience and diligence are needed to partake of the fruit that this book has to offer. Furthermore, it necessitates a disposition of kenosis or a state of self-emptiness, for as the saying goes, "Empty your cup so that it may be filled." If you are of the opinion that your cup is already full, then you cannot experience growth or advancement. Hence, another consequence of truth is that it leaves you in a better position than you were previously. Truth always provides a greater value than what was previously enjoyed or experienced. Truth does not deprive.

2 Timothy 2:15 says, "Study to shew thyself approved unto God, a workman that needeth not to be ashamed, rightly dividing the word of truth." As with most disciplines, there are specific rules that have to be followed to attain mastery. For example, world-class athletes subject themselves to a regimented life to become proficient at their craft.

As it pertains to the Word of God, to have a correct interpretation of Scripture, the principles of rightly dividing the Word have to be adhered to. As I mentioned in my book, *The Volume of the Book: Insights into Rightly Dividing the Word of God*, interpretation of the Scripture is more of a science than an art. Most things associated with the concept of "art" allow improvisations, creative injections, and feelings. They are concerned with reasoning and follow a more liberal and subjective approach. On the other hand, studies connected with "science" abide by a more specific framework and are more definite and objective. In practical terms, it is often said that cooking is an art, whereas baking is a science. While cooking allows you more latitude to make it up as you go along, baking requires complying with more precise measurements.

As a parallel, providing enlightenment concerning women in ministry, like baking, mandates following clear principles or a "scientific approach" rather than an arbitrary method.

As a student of Scripture driven by these principles, I use every opportunity to include them while commenting on various topics. In this regard, the fundamentals of context and perspective of Scripture will be the first two principles considered. In general terms, in order to have the proper perspective of Scripture, it requires having the proper context of Scripture. Our perspective on particular subjects is sometimes incorrect because our context regarding these matters is faulty. In harmony with this discussion, for there to be an accurate perspective regarding women in ministry, the proper context of Scripture first has to be established. Again, many times, our interpretations or points-of-view are incorrect because our context is skewed. *Therefore, proper context results in proper perspective.*

    Proper Context   ═══   Proper Perspective

The Context of Scripture

Context, as it pertains to Scripture, means the following:

- The inter-related conditions in which Scripture exists or occurs
- The circumstances or settings in which an event in Scripture occurs. Also, the conditions and circumstances that are relevant to the verse or passage
- The part of a text or statement (passage) that surrounds a particular word or verse and determines its meaning
- The scripture that precedes and follows a verse or passage and contributes to its full meaning or influences its meaning or effect
- The set of circumstances or facts that surround a particular verse, passage, book, or testament

According to the definitions of the word "context," when studying the Scriptures, it is imperative to take into account not only, the verse being considered but also the environment in which the verse exists. The principle, therefore, dictates that the verse or passage cannot be viewed in isolation but must be seen based on its setting. Hence, consideration has to be given to the circumstances in which the verse occurs. Furthermore, what was said before the verse and what is yet to be said have to be taken into account. When verses of Scripture are used separately to stand alone and independent of the context, this results in fragments of the context and an incorrect perspective. Within the scope of the context of Scripture, there are four constituents that must be applied to understand Scripture correctly. As I pointed out, the scriptural resolution concerning women in ministry requires a detailed systematic approach.

Principles for the Context of Scripture

- **The Passage Context:** Verses of a particular chapter must not be interpreted in isolation from the chapter, passage, or book under consideration. A passage context includes all the verses and chapters of a particular book, which focus on a specific subject.
- **The Book Context:** Each book of the Bible has a central theme running through its chapters. The context of the verse has to be considered within the context of the entire book in which it is found.
- **The Testament Context:** Each Testament of the Bible has a general context. The general theme of the Old Testament is Law and the general theme of the New Testament is grace. The verse or passage being considered has to be examined in the context of the Testament in which it exists.
- **The Volume of the Book or Whole of Scripture Context:** To get the context on a particular subject, all scriptures pertaining to the topic have to be examined.

As you can determine, study not only requires adherence to principles, but it also takes time and dedication. I reiterate, once the proper context has been established, then a proper perspective can be achieved. Doctrine cannot be based on one scripture but rather on the reconciliation of all scriptures regarding a particular subject matter.

The Perspective of Scripture

In plain language, perspective simply means, the particular way we look or think about something.

Perspective as it pertains to Scripture means:

- To see the Scriptures as God intends for them to be seen or from His point-of-view
- To ensure that all passages of Scripture used are in true relationship with the whole of Scripture
- The capacity to view Scripture in its true relation or relative importance.
- To see the Scriptures in their true relationship.

In accordance with the definition of "perspective," it is apparent that in order to have the proper perspective of Scripture, it is essential to examine the relationship the scriptures share with each other. With that said, while using these principles, we will examine some of the scriptures, which speak specifically concerning women in ministry.

At the conclusion of this exercise, the following questions will be adequately addressed with the hope that all ambiguity regarding women in ministry will be eliminated.

- Can women be pastors or function in church leadership?
- What does Scripture say about women speaking in the church? Are they to be silent or are they restricted to teaching Sunday school, singing, reading the announcements, or performing other auxiliary responsibilities?
- Is gender a factor in the kingdom of God?

- What is the difference between a woman functioning in a marriage environment and in a kingdom setting or the church?
- Does a woman need a male as a covering to function in a leadership role in the church?
- Can women teach/preach in the church?
- What does it mean to usurp authority over a man or have a Jezebel spirit?
- Do women need to have their heads covered in order to prophesy or function in ministry?

THE CONTEXT AND PERSPECTIVE OF 1 CORINTHIANS

Women Speaking in the Church

While organizing my notes for this book, Vanria Edwards, a friend of mine, sent me a video of a man who, while teaching, was vehemently opposed to women speaking in the church on any level. The way he paraded on stage while quoting Scripture seemed nothing short of an intimidation tactic. Having attended a seminar I conducted a few weeks prior, she understood my position on the subject and wanted to know my thoughts on the video. After watching the thirty-minute clip in its entirety, I had a basket of mixed emotions and responses.

First, I felt repulsed, not just by the words he used but also by the tone of his delivery. Not only did he disagree with women in ministry, but he also sounded disagreeable. Additionally, I felt a degree of remorse for those in the audience who were subjected to such teaching. Finally, I felt a sense of obligation and responsibility to offer the truth of the Scriptures to set people free from the bondage of religious oppression and ignorance. Among others, one of the scriptures he used was 1 Corinthians 14:34-35.

> 34. Let your women keep silence in the churches: for it is not permitted unto them to speak; but they are commanded to be under obedience, as also saith the law.
> 35. And if they will learn anything, let them ask their husbands at home: for it is a shame for women to speak in the church. (1 Corinthians 14:34-35)

In reconciling this passage, some of the traditional perspectives promulgated by the church are as follows:

- During this time, women were being disruptive; therefore, they had to be silenced.
- This measure had to be taken to maintain order in the church.
- Back then, women were unlearned. Therefore, asking their husbands at home was acceptable so as not to disturb the assembly.
- The outright position that women are not permitted to speak in the church.

Obviously, the first two opinions are biased assumptions improperly characterizing women, while, at the same time, excluding the tendencies of men. To conclude that irregular behavior is limited specifically to one gender is illogical and has a misogynist undertone. Moreover, many proponents of women ministers or women speaking in the church offer the first three points as reasonable explanations for the passage. Furthermore, they conclude that since these conditions no longer exist, there is now justification for women speaking in the church.

Specifically, in relation to the third point, with women being more educated today, the rationale is that this stipulation no longer applies. The challenge with this premise is that when we submit ourselves to subjective reasoning as opposed to the truth of Scripture, the conclusions are susceptible to varying conditions. This often results in debates and not an objective standard of truth. Concerning the fourth point, this is the position of those who adamantly oppose women speaking in the church.

Despite the reasoning of the first three points, the assessment of 1 Corinthians 14:34-35 held by many is that women are not permitted to speak or teach in the church but are to remain silent. This is further compounded with the inclusion that it is a shame for a woman to speak in the church. With debates surrounding this scripture being mostly based on conjecture, we are left with a subjective point of view. However, the best approach to understanding this passage is to allow Scripture to interpret Scripture. By taking opinions out of the equation, we are left with an objective standard of truth by which everything is to be weighed.

Of all the passages, I find that this is certainly one of the more popular scriptures used in opposition to women speaking in the church, being ministers, or having a leading role in the church. However, what I find ironic is that even in some churches that subscribe to this conviction, women are not totally silent. Instead, they are assigned to seemingly "secondary" roles. These include assignments such as Sunday school teachers, psalmists, announcements, or auxiliary responsibilities. In this regard, these allocations, though probably patronizing, are done so that women are not excluded altogether and feel less marginalized. For if the word "silence" is held in absolute then even these gestures would be contrary to the common interpretation of this scripture.

Reconciliation of 1 Corinthians 14:34-35

In reconciling this passage of Scripture, we have to ask the following questions:

- What is the correct perspective based on the context of the book of 1 Corinthians?
- Based on the "whole of Scripture context," what is the reconciliation of this passage?
- What if the woman is not married?
- Is the Law the prevailing constituent in this discussion?

Most New Testament books are also referred to as epistles or letters. When reading them, this format has to be taken into account. For instance, if you received a letter of approximately sixteen pages like 1 Corinthians, is it your normal practice to immediately read page fourteen and have a precise understanding of what is being communicated? Of course not! Perhaps a certain premise was submitted in the early portion of the letter that laid the foundation for what would be said later in the correspondence. Therefore, when page fourteen is read, the perspective would already be understood. For example, upon receiving a letter from your girlfriend, you skim through portions of the letter, and you notice on page nine that she says she "loves you." However, unbeknownst to you, this is like the song in which someone says, "I love you to say goodbye." Nevertheless, you totally missed her perspective because you failed to read the full content of the letter. In fact, on page five of the letter, she states the multiple reasons why you can no longer be together. She gives the classic, "It's not you; it's me" explanation. However, by directing all your attention to page nine of the letter, the context is missed altogether and instead, you buy her flowers and a ring.

In creating a parallel with 1 Corinthians, is it fitting to simply read a portion of Chapter 14 of the letter and draw conclusions about the context of the entire epistle? Recall that when the context of a verse or passage is being considered, the overall context or the "book context" has to be weighed. Following this principle eliminates any contradiction between the verse or passage and the general theme of the entire book.

What is the central theme running through the chapters of 1 Corinthians? What is the purpose of the book?

The Context of the Book of 1 Corinthians

Corinth, formerly a territory of Greece, was a major city in the Roman province of Achaia during the time Paul established the church there. In his capacity as an apostle, Paul addressed the letter to the church at Corinth, and in the fashion of a letter, he opens with a salutation.

1. Paul, called to be an apostle of Jesus Christ through the will of God, and Sosthenes our brother,
2. Unto the church of God which is at Corinth, to them that are sanctified in Christ Jesus, called to be saints, with all that in every place call upon the name of Jesus Christ our Lord, both theirs and ours:
3. Grace be unto you, and peace, from God our Father, and from the Lord Jesus Christ. (1 Corinthians 1:1-3)

In principle, the letter was designed to address concerns regarding the conduct, beliefs, and practices of the members of the church. It was also to establish doctrine concerning specific subjects. However, in terms of structure, the epistle is a <u>response</u> to two distinct matters.

The first portion of the letter was written in response to a report Paul received from the members of the house of Chloe (1 Corinthians 1:11), along with other reports. Hence, members of Chloe's house and others sent communication informing him of the things that were going on in the church. For the purpose of this discussion, this was the "unofficial report" that was sent to Paul. Therefore, from Chapter 1 to Chapter 6, Paul addresses these matters, which were brought to his attention.

The second portion of 1 Corinthians was written in response to the letter the church of Corinth sent to Paul (1 Corinthians

7:1). This was the "official" letter the Corinthians sent to Paul that ironically didn't include the other "unofficial" matters that were sent by Choe's household and others. The Corinthians had several matters they needed instruction on; hence, they sent Paul a letter with those petitions in order to receive answers. Let us look at the two components of the letter in detail.

The Report from Chloe's Household and Other Reports

As mentioned, members of the house of Chloe informed Paul of certain activities that were present in the Corinthian church. This is acknowledged in 1 Corinthians 1:11.

> For it hath been declared unto me of you, my brethren, by them which are of the house of Chloe, that there are contentions among you. (1 Corinthians 1:11)

Additionally, other reports were brought to Paul's attention regarding matters in the church. For example, in 1 Corinthians 5:1 he says,

> It is reported commonly that there is fornication among you, and such fornication as is not so much as named among the Gentiles, that one should have his father's wife.

In the first six chapters of 1 Corinthians, Paul addresses these matters of the church that were brought to his attention. Below is a complete list of the concerns presented to him.

- In the church of Corinth, there were divisions and contentions (1 Corinthians 1:10-11). This threatened the unity and growth of the church. Some indicated that they were of Paul; others aligned themselves with Apollos; another group said they were of Cephas (Peter) and the remainder identified themselves with Christ (1 Corinthians 1:12).
- Based on this scenario, Paul, in 1 Corinthians Chapter 3, not only offers the message of unity but also provides the proper perspective of ministry and the work of ministers. The principle is that despite the individual work of ministers, God is the One who provides the increase or spiritual growth. Hence, the focus is always on God and not on individual ministers.
- After addressing the reports from the house of Chloe, Paul then turns his attention to the other matters that were presented to him. In 1 Corinthians 5, he responds to the reports of fornication in the church. Specifically, he cites the scenario where a man was involved with his father's wife. In fact, he even makes the point that such a manner of fornication was not being mentioned among unbelievers.
- Finally, in addressing the matters that were brought to his attention, Paul tables the issue of believers taking each other to court in order to resolve legal matters (1 Corinthians 6:1-8). Instead, he admonishes them to present their concerns before wise believers. To add perspective to this point, he says that in the age to come, believers will judge both the world and angels. Based on this premise, Paul exhorts them to resolve matters of justice between themselves.

What I find interesting is that 1 Corinthians reveals typical church behavior similar to what exists today. When the Corinthians wrote the "official" letter to Paul, these concerns were obviously not included. Isn't it amazing that the matters pertaining to the inner workings of the heart and righteous behavior are seldom presented for discussion in comparison to other topics? Fortunately, those from the house of Chloe and others furnished reports on the "other" challenges that were facing the church.

Responses to the Letter Received From the Corinthian Church

After addressing the report from Chloe's household, along with the other reports he received, Paul turns his attention to the details of the letter that the Corinthian church wrote to him. This is acknowledged in 1 Corinthians 7:1:

> Now concerning the things whereof ye wrote unto me. (1 Corinthians 7:1)

As I mentioned before, the church at Corinth had been recently established and the members had questions regarding specific spiritual matters and church functions. Hence, they wrote Paul a letter for him to address their queries. In responding to them, he dedicates the second portion of 1 Corinthians to answer the various subjects contained in their letter. As a point of reference, the occasion of the church writing a letter to Paul was not unprecedented as the church at Laodicea also wrote Paul a letter. They shared correspondence as communication was bilateral.

> And when this epistle is read among you, cause that it be read also in the church of the Laodiceans; and that ye likewise read the epistle from Laodicea. (Colossians 4:16)

In addition, this example gives us the general premise that although the epistles were originally directed to a particular church, they were also meant for other churches. In truth, they were intended for the entire body of Christ. Furthermore, it also demonstrates that letters were written as a means of dialogue between the members and church leadership. Hence, in the case of 1 Corinthians, from Chapter 7 to the end of the letter, what we really have is a dialogue between Paul and the church of Corinth. However, it is imperative to distinguish the items presented by the church and the responses provided by Paul. Often, in responding to a particular subject, he first restates their query and then provides a response. Therefore, the entire letter of 1 Corinthians is a combination of what the church says in their letter and Paul's responses.

As we progress through the letter, Paul addresses their inquiries in a distinguishable fashion. In making his responses easier to identify, he begins most of the subjects with either the words, "now concerning," or "now as." This basically serves as a marker from one topic to the next. The general subjects in relation to their letter are listed below.

1. TOUCHING A WOMAN AND THE DYNAMICS OF MARRIAGE

1. <u>Now concerning the things whereof ye wrote unto me: It is good for a man not to touch a woman.</u>

> 2. Nevertheless, to avoid fornication, let every man have his own wife, and let every woman have her own husband. (1 Corinthians 7:1-2)

The first matter tabled by Paul based on the letter he received from the Corinthian church pertained to inappropriate touching and marriage. Therefore, he takes the opportunity to address the subject of marriage as a means of avoiding fornication. Additionally, he offers guidelines concerning a husband and wife relationship.

2. VIRGINS OR BEING UNMARRIED

> <u>Now concerning virgins</u> I have no commandment of the Lord: yet I give my judgment, as one that hath obtained mercy of the Lord to be faithful. (1 Corinthians 7:25)

The second matter presented to Paul by the Corinthian church pertained to virgins or being unmarried in relation to doing the work of the Lord. Therefore, for the remainder of 1 Corinthians Chapter 7, he presents the dynamics involved in being a virgin or an unmarried person versus being married. Notwithstanding his reference to the "present distress," Paul offers a meaningful perspective concerning the subject.

> 32. But I would have you without carefulness. He that is unmarried careth for the things that belong to the Lord, how he may please the Lord:

> 33. But he that is married careth for the things that are of the world, how he may please his wife.
> 34. There is difference also between a wife and a virgin. The unmarried woman careth for the things of the Lord, that she may be holy both in body and in spirit: but she that is married careth for the things of the world, how she may please her husband. (1 Corinthians 7:32-34)

Hence, he concludes that remaining unmarried allows you to do the work of the Lord without distraction. To this end, he says that he wishes everyone were unmarried like him. However, he also understands that not everyone has the gift of celibacy.

3. THINGS OFFERED TO IDOLS

> <u>Now as touching things offered unto idols</u>, we know that we all have knowledge. (1 Corinthians 8:1)

The third subject submitted to Paul by the church at Corinth was whether it was appropriate for believers to partake of meat that had been offered or sacrificed to idols. In addressing this point, Paul establishes a foundation in 1 Corinthians 8:4:

> As concerning therefore the eating of those things that are offered in the sacrifice unto idols, we

> know that an idol is nothing in the world, and that there is none other God but one.

In responding to their query, Paul attributes the Corinthians with knowing that an idol is nothing and that there is only one true God. He says, "You have this knowledge." However, he makes the distinction that despite having this awareness, they should also be cognizant that not everyone is equipped with this same understanding. Therefore, while partaking of food offered to idols has no real significance, the liberty of those with this knowledge could defile those who are weak by their actions. Hence, based on this premise, Paul submits in 1 Corinthians 8:13 that "If meat make my brother to offend, I will eat no flesh while the world standeth, lest I make my brother to offend." This act is truly a demonstration of love and exemplifies the statement made in 1 Corinthians 8:1 that knowledge puffs up but charity or love edifies.

After offering instructions on things offered unto idols, Paul in 1 Corinthians Chapter 9 turns his attention to the subject of his apostolic authority. He uses the chapter to certify his apostleship of the church and his qualification to provide the responses to their letter. He determined this was necessary because some people questioned his authority. Apparently, the validity of his office was under scrutiny by some in the church, so he dedicated this chapter to address this and other matters.

> 1. Am I not an apostle? am I not free? have I not seen Jesus Christ our Lord? are not ye my work in the Lord?

2. If I be not an apostle unto others, yet doubtless I am to you: for the seal of mine apostleship are ye in the Lord
3. Mine answer to them that do examine me is this. (1 Corinthians 9:1-3)

Subsequent to his discussion on food offered to idols in 1 Corinthians Chapter 8, Paul provides an additional perspective on the subject in 1 Corinthians Chapter 10. However, he broadens the conversation to include a discussion on idolatry. Therefore, in admonishing the church to flee from idolatry, Paul uses the example of Israel's idolatry while in the wilderness. In the chapter, he creates a parallel between Israel and the church. He points out that despite Israel having spiritual meat and spiritual drink, after they partook of them, they still turned to idolatry (Exodus 32:19). The spiritual meat in the passage refers to the manna that fell from heaven (Exodus 16:13-15) and the spiritual drink speaks of the water, which came from the rock that Moses struck (Exodus 17:5-6). Moreover, in furthering the parallel, Paul says that the manna (bread) and the drink had spiritual significance because they represented partaking of Jesus Christ. Consequently, they both depicted the communion or partaking of Christ's body and blood. However, even though they were figuratively partaking of Christ or partaking of the Lord's Table, afterward, they still engaged in idolatry (Exodus 32). "1 Corinthians 10:7 says, "The people sat down to eat and drink, and rose up to play." Hence, the chapter is creating a contrast between two distinct tables and two types of fellowships.

In making the connection to food offered to idols, Paul states that the food offered to idols is sacrificed to devils, not to God; therefore, partaking of such food represents eating at the Devil's table and having fellowship with devils. Conversely, when believers partake of the Lord's supper, this represents partaking of the Lord's table and having fellowship with the Lord. Based on this premise, Paul offers a conclusion in 1 Corinthians 10:21, "Ye cannot drink the cup of the Lord, and the cup of devils: ye cannot be partakers of the Lord's Table, and of the table of devils."

In summary, he states that it is only from the Lord's Table that believers should be partaking. Moreover, Paul says that to eliminate offending anyone, if you are invited to a feast, do not ask if the food was offered to idols. However, if it is stated that the food was offered to idols, do not partake in consideration of the conscience of those who are weak.

1 Corinthians Chapter 11 speaks to the subject of God's divine order and covering. However, this will be addressed as a separate topic in Chapter 4 of this book.

4. SPIRITUAL GIFTS

The next item on the docket in terms of Paul's responses to the Corinthian church is the matter of spiritual gifts. Of all the topics that Paul responds to, this is certainly one of the more comprehensive as three chapters of 1 Corinthians are dedicated to adequately addressing this subject. In addition to the other points contained in the letter that he received from the Corinthian church was the matter of spiritual gifts. Hence, Paul begins His response in 1 Corinthians Chapter 12 with,

<u>Now concerning spiritual gifts</u>, brethren, I would not have you ignorant. (1 Corinthians 12:1)

In the chapter, while focusing on spiritual gifts, Paul underscores the subject by establishing the message of unity and equality. He asserts that regardless of diversity or differences, unity still exists. Two examples are used to support this. First, as it pertains to spiritual gifts, 1 Corinthians 12:4-7 says that even though there are diversities of gifts, differences in administration, and distinctions of operation, it is <u>the same Spirit who works them</u>, giving to every man as He wills. Furthermore, the communication of unity and equality in the body of Christ is expressed by using the illustration of the human body.

It submits that despite having many members, the body is still one. Hence, the message throughout the chapter is consistent—unity despite differences. Additionally, in this conveyance of unity and equality, to avoid division, it also adds that just as the human body requires all members in order to function, so does the body of Christ. No member of the body is to be dismissed or made to feel insignificant. Please note that 1 Corinthians 12 to 14 represent a "passage context" on the operation of spiritual gifts in the church. *Therefore, this foundation of unity and equality in the body sets the stage for everything else that will be discussed concerning spiritual gifts.*

In continuing with the discussion on spiritual gifts and the admonition to desire them, 1 Corinthians Chapter 13 begins with the principle that even if we function in the gifts and do not have love, it is useless.

> Though I speak with the tongues of men and of angles, and have not charity, I am become

as sounding brass, or a tinkling cymbal. (1 Corinthians 13:1)

Furthermore, the chapter conveys the message that despite functioning in the gifts and making tremendous sacrifices, without love there is no benefit to our efforts.

After expounding on the principle of love in relation to the gifts in 1 Corinthians Chapter 13, the conversation of spiritual gifts is continued in 1 Corinthians Chapter 14. 1 Corinthians 14:1 says, "Follow after charity (love), and desire spiritual gifts, but rather that ye may prophesy." The chapter then makes the distinction between speaking in unknown tongues compared to prophesying, along with the purpose and benefits of each. For the benefit of this discussion, unknown tongues are for speaking to God and self-edification because no one can understand what is being said (1 Corinthians 14:14). On the other hand, known tongues are actually other (known) languages: English, French, Spanish, Japanese, etc., used to convey the message of God to people of different languages. Therefore, the chapter draws a contrast between speaking in unknown tongues, which only edifies the individual compared to prophesying (which includes teaching) that brings edification, exhortation, and comfort to the entire body. Based on this distinction, Paul says that in the church, he "would rather speak five words with my understanding that by my voice I might teach others than ten thousand words in an unknown tongue." In other words, he would prefer to offer instruction in a language that people could understand and benefit from as opposed to unknown tongues that no one understands.

Apparently, there was an abundance of people speaking in

unknown tongues in the church, but the body was not being edified. Hence, the call was for things to be done orderly in the church. Thus, the chapter emphasizes, "Forasmuch as ye are zealous of spiritual gifts, seek that ye may excel to the edifying of the church" (1 Corinthians 14:12). This same sentiment is echoed as the conversation progresses to how things should be conducted regarding other elements of corporate worship.

> How is it then, brethren? when ye come together, every one of you hath a psalm, hath a doctrine, hath a tongue, hath a revelation, hath an interpretation. <u>Let all things be done unto edifying.</u> (1 Corinthians 14:26)

Just as it is with unknown tongues and prophesying (speaking in a known tongue), where the principal thing is the edification of the church, so it is with the various contributions of believers during joint fellowship. This is particularly relevant to speaking in an unknown tongue and having someone interpret what was said so believers could be edified and order maintained. Hence, in his communication about spiritual gifts, Paul establishes the parameters in which they should function. To this end, 1 Corinthians 14:33 provides the principle that God is not the author of confusion but of peace.

I know for many this method of resolution regarding the subject of women speaking in the church may seem taxing or labourious. However, it is the absence of such systematic teaching, which has resulted in the misinterpretation of Scripture.

Please be mindful that the subject matter of 1 Corinthians

Chapter 14 is not specifically women speaking in the church. Rather, as we have established based on the passage context, it is spiritual gifts along with prophesying. Therefore, during the discussion of prophesying and orderliness during corporate fellowship, the matter of women prophesying or teaching in the church is also introduced.

As we have established, the letter of 1 Corinthians represents a dialogue between Paul and the Corinthian church for instruction on specific matters. As portions of the letter are in an exchange format, if it was written in the days of instant messaging like we have today, the communication concerning women speaking in the church would look something like this.

> 34. Let your women keep silence in the churches: for it is not permitted unto them to speak; but they are commanded to be under obedience, as also saith the law.
> 35. And if they will learn anything, let them ask their husbands at home: for it is a shame for women to speak in the church. (1 Corinthians 14:34-35)

> 36. What? came the word of God out from you? or came it unto you only? (1 Corinthians 14:36)

Notice that after the verses on women speaking in the church, Paul provides an immediate response. Hence, verses 34 and 35 represent the position that the church submitted in their letter and verse 36 outlines Paul's response. His expression is an abrupt "what?!"

According to the *Urban Dictionary*, this reaction is rhetorical and is asked to undermine someone's point or position. In everyday language, it is the same as, "I can't believe you just said that." It also means, "That doesn't make sense or that's not relevant." This is followed by two additional questions to the church. "Came the word of God out from you only? Or came it to you only?" In other words, as the Amplified Bible puts it, he was asking them, "Did the word of God originate with you?" "Has it come to you only?"

In simple language, Paul was asking them, "Are you the ones responsible for establishing the doctrine of the church, particularly concerning women speaking in the church?" Certainly, these same questions can be asked of denominations or churches that oppose women in ministry today. Combined, his responses serve as a rebuke based on the query the church presented to him. Paul's general sentiment is, "How dare you think that men are the only ones capable of prophesying in the church, or is the Word of God only meant for your benefit?"

In particular, the challenge many have with these verses is two-fold. First, as previously mentioned, whenever our context concerning a matter is incorrect, our perspectives are subsequently inaccurate. Hence, not knowing the context of the book and its dialogue format, the misconception is that the entire letter represents a solitary communication from Paul to the church. Second, with preconceived notions already established regarding women speaking in the church, after reading verses 34 and 35, no consideration is given to the verses that follow. The grave error is that the verses are read in isolation without considering the relationship they have with the other verses or with the overall context of the book.

After providing clarification on the matter, particularly, as it pertains to women prophesying or teaching in the church, he assures the church he is writing the commandments of the Lord. However, he adds that those who persist in remaining ignorant concerning this matter are free to do so. Nevertheless, let proper manners and order prevail in the church.

> 37. If any man think himself to be a prophet, or spiritual, let him acknowledge that the things that I write unto you are the commandments of the Lord.
> 38. But if any man be ignorant, let him be ignorant.
> 39. Wherefore, brethren, covet to prophesy, and forbid not to speak with tongues.
> 40. Let all things be done decently and in order.
> (1 Corinthians 14:37-40)

Notice that to support their query of women being silent in the church, the Corinthian church used the Law to substantiate their position. First, this reference was not applicable because the church is not subjected to the general tenets of the Law. Additionally, their specific reference to the Law was based on the judgment of Genesis 3:16, where the husband became the head of his wife. However, as we have determined, this judgment pertained to a family setting and the relationship between a husband and his wife.

With that said, they were attempting to apply this judgment to the operation of the church as many churches do today. Nevertheless, this application does not take into consideration the distinction between a family environment and a kingdom environment. Moreover, the statement, "as also saith the Law," gives no consideration to the church being under the dispensation of grace. Therefore, such an inclusion was irrelevant. Furthermore, their position that a wife should wait until she got home to ask her husband questions concerning matters she learned at church does not account for women who are not married. Recall that Paul encouraged being unmarried in Chapter 7. Therefore, if he promotes being single to do the work of the Lord without distraction, how does this scenario apply to women who are single? Based on their misguided interpretation of the Scripture, Paul's scathing rebuke was a completely justifiable response. He said "What? Did the word of God originate with you?"

5. THE COLLECTION FOR THE SAINTS

The fifth and final subject presented to Paul by the Corinthian church pertained to the collection for the saints. He addresses this concern in 1 Corinthians Chapter 16.

> <u>Now concerning the collection for the saints</u>, as I have given order to the churches of Galatia, even so do ye. (1 Corinthians 16:1)

Notice now that we have a better appreciation for the context of 1 Corinthians, the perspective, particularly in reference to women speaking in the church is totally different. As opposed to subjective reasonings to determine an understanding of 1 Corinthians 14:34-35, the Scripture was allowed to interpret itself. As a result, we have an objective standard of truth, which can withstand the test of varying opinions.

In following the principles of rightly dividing the Word of God, our conclusion of 1 Corinthians Chapter 14 was not based on that chapter alone, but rather it was in accordance with the context of the entire book of 1 Corinthians. This allowed us to take a systematic approach to understand the dialogue format of the book and properly follow its communication. Hence, Paul never said that women should be silent in the church but was simply addressing the query presented to him by the church. Consequently, his response was in total contradiction of the position they submitted.

This same systematic principle utilized in this chapter will be applied for the next discussion on covering for women.

COVERING FOR WOMEN

Wearing Hats

As a youngster in the Baptist church, I can vividly recall women always wearing hats or some form of covering on their heads while speaking in the church. On one occasion, I even observed a woman borrowing a hat from another woman in order to fulfill a speaking role due to a change in the church's program. Additionally, I heard 1 Corinthians 11:5 repeatedly quoted by those in leadership. Consequently, it was ingrained in my mind that Scripture mandated the covering of women's heads when they are engaged in speaking assignments in the church.

> But every woman that prayeth or prophesieth with her head uncovered dishonoureth her head: for that is even all one as if she were shaven. (1 Corinthians 11:5)

I must admit that the evolution of hats has taken us into the stratosphere of fashion as the creativity involved in their preparation is astounding. In fact, during the Baptist Day Parades in the Bahamas, the hats are a separate conversation piece; the display rivals the runways of the latest fashion shows. It is my prayer that those who are engaged in hat production, specifically for women in the church, and who depend on it for their livelihood, continue to thrive. However, with the fruit of truth being freedom, this chapter is intended for those who feel compelled to wear a hat while speaking in the church, as well as for those who scrutinize the women who do not. My hope is that at the end of this chapter, women who choose to wear a hat or covering while praying or prophesying, will be able to do so from the position of liberty or strictly as an adornment, rather than out of religious obligation.

Later in life, when I transitioned to another church under the banner of "non-denominational," I noticed the women in that setting wore no hats. Admittedly, at first, I thought this was unconventional considering my background, but eventually, I accepted the change, especially with the Pentecostal departure from "tradition." Nevertheless, despite my new way of thinking, whenever I read 1 Corinthians Chapter 11, I still could not thoroughly explain my new conviction. Again, I say it is challenging having a persuasion in support of or in opposition to a matter and not be able to validate the position with Scripture.

Having already established the context for the book of 1 Corinthians, that it is essentially a dialogue between Paul and the church at Corinth, the perspective of 1 Corinthians Chapter 11 can also be appreciated based on this premise. While tabling the matters that were presented to him for instruction, Paul also takes the opportunity to create a comparison between the traditions he established with the church and the ones that existed at Corinth.

Based on a misinterpretation of this chapter, the church has created a religious identity and culture with a custom that women are required to wear hats while praying or prophesying. Furthermore, with the topic of headship, the chapter is also used as a basis for gender suppression, and women, in general, are made to feel inferior to men.

2. Now I praise you, brethren, that ye remember me in all things, and keep the ordinances, as I delivered them to you.
3. But I would have you know, that the head of every man is Christ; and the head of the woman is the man; and the head of Christ is God.
4. Every man praying or prophesying, having his head covered, dishonoureth his head.
5. But every woman that prayeth or prophesieth with her head uncovered dishonoureth her head: for that is even all one as if she were shaven.
6. For if the woman be not covered, let her also be shorn: but if it be a shame for a

woman to be shorn or shaven, let her be covered.

7. For a man indeed ought not to cover his head, forasmuch as he is the image and glory of God: but the woman is the glory of the man.
8. For the man is not of the woman; but the woman of the man.
9. Neither was the man created for the woman; but the woman for the man.
10. For this cause ought the woman to have power on her head because of the angels.
11. Nevertheless neither is the man without the woman, neither the woman without the man, in the Lord.
12. For as the woman is of the man, even so is the man also by the woman; but all things of God.
13. Judge in yourselves: is it comely that a woman pray unto God uncovered?
14. Doth not even nature itself teach you, that, if a man have long hair, it is a shame unto him?
15. But if a woman have long hair, it is a glory to her: for her hair is given her for a covering.
16. But if any man seem to be contentious, we have no such custom, neither the churches of God. (1 Corinthians 11:2-16)

Before beginning the discussion, I wish to create a parallel between the above passage and the one of the previous chapter regarding women speaking in the church. If we hold onto the persuasion that women are to be silent in the church or are not permitted to prophesy in the church (1 Corinthians 14:34-35), how is it that in 1 Corinthians Chapter 11, it gives credence to women prophesying or teaching (in the church), as long as their heads are covered? Note that both verses are contained in the same letter. Obviously, prophesying requires speaking so this seems to contradict the message of 1 Corinthians 14:35-35. Nevertheless, as the matter of women speaking in the church has already been resolved, there is no ambiguity here. As the subject of 1 Corinthians Chapter 11 involves prophecy and covering, they will be addressed separately.

Prophecy and Prophesying

In the body of Christ, we seem to have the notion that the ability to prophesy only pertains to speaking regarding future events. However, the word "prophesy" actually means to speak by divine inspiration, which also includes teaching. Recall from the previous chapter that the purpose of prophecy is for edification, exhortation, and comfort (1 Corinthians 14:3). To have a better perspective of what prophecy entails, let us look at the definitions of prophecy and prophesying.

Prophecy and Prophesying Defined

The word "prophecy" is the Greek word *propheteia* and it means the following:

- To speak by divine inspiration, declaring the purposes of God whether by reproving and admonishing the wicked, comforting the afflicted, or revealing things hidden, especially by foretelling future events

The word "prophesying" is the Greek word *propheteuo* and it means the following:

- To predict or foretell future events, especially pertaining to the kingdom of God
- To declare truths by the inspiration of God's Holy Spirit, whether by prediction or not
- To declare a thing, which can only be known by divine revelation
- To teach or admonish others

Therefore, based on the definitions and their function in Scripture, prophecy is not limited to forecasting events but also involves teaching for the purpose of edifying the church. Furthermore, based on the gifts of the Holy Spirit mentioned in 1 Corinthians Chapter 12, prophecy also encompasses the word of knowledge and the word of wisdom. In short, the word of knowledge speaks to obtaining specific information about something or someone that was not obtained by natural means. As it is based on facts or information, it is not intended to provide a directive (Matthew 16:13-17). The word of wisdom, on the other hand, involves divine insight on what should be done in a particular situation (Acts 27:10-30). Therefore, prophecy is comprehensive in that it is not limited to one specific thing.

Joel 2:28-29 outlines a prophecy foretelling that the Lord will pour out His Spirit upon all flesh. Notice it says that because of this, *both men and women shall be able to prophesy.*

28. And it shall come to pass afterward, that I will pour out my spirit upon all flesh; <u>and your sons and your daughters shall prophesy,</u> your old men shall dream dreams, your young men shall see visions:

29. And also upon the <u>servants and upon the handmaids</u> in those days will I pour out my spirit. (Joel 2:28-29)

In support of Joel's prophecy, clearly, it was the Lord's intent for women to also prophesy, which includes teaching. For if this was not His intent for women, then they would have been excluded from this prophecy. This prophecy was fulfilled in Acts Chapter 2 on the Day of Pentecost when the Holy Ghost filled the apostles and disciples (which included women). Peter, therefore, confirms this in Acts 2:14-18.

14. But Peter, standing up with the eleven, lifted up his voice, and said unto them, Ye men of Judaea, and all ye that dwell at Jerusalem, be this known unto you, and hearken to my words:

15. For these are not drunken, as ye suppose, seeing it is but the third hour of the day.

16. But this is that which was spoken by the prophet Joel;

17. And it shall come to pass in the last days, saith God, I will pour out of my Spirit upon all flesh: and your sons and your daughters shall prophesy, and your young men shall see visions, and your old men shall dream dreams:

> 18. And on my servants and on my handmaidens
> I will pour out in those days of my Spirit; and
> they shall prophesy. (Acts 2:14-18)

Notice that as a result of being filled with the Holy Ghost, they began to speak <u>with other tongues</u> as the Spirit gave them utterance. Recall that Joel referred to this as <u>prophesying</u>. Specifically, they were not speaking in unknown tongues but rather, known tongues or languages. Despite being from Galilee, they were speaking in the language of the Parthians, Medes, Egyptians, Asians, Cretans, Arabians, etc. In the language of various nations present at Jerusalem, they were speaking the wonderful works of God (Acts 2:5-11). Hence, as the example affirms, the ability to prophesy also includes the ability to speak concerning the goodness of God or teach.

Now that we have discussed what it means to prophesy, let us continue with the context of 1 Corinthians Chapter 11 and head covering.

Reconciling Scripture Regarding Head Covering

Before specifically addressing the subject of head covering, Paul begins the chapter by admonishing the church to keep the traditions or ordinances he gave them.

> Now I praise you, brethren, that ye remember me
> in all things, and keep the ordinances, as I delivered them to you. (1 Corinthians 11:2)

In simple terms, the word "ordinance" means a body of precepts, teachings, or instructions. Therefore, he says to the church, "I gave you some traditions or ordinances that I want you to keep."

Many times, when we think of traditions, the normal tendency of the church is to reflect on ineffective activities. However, in this instance, the traditions Paul was referring to were instructions for righteous living mentioned previously throughout the letter. For example, this included being of the same mind, in unity, and without divisions (1 Corinthians 1:10). It also focused on dealing with sexual immorality and the effects of sin (1 Corinthians Chapter 5). It incorporated teachings on marriage and fornication (1 Corinthians Chapter 7). Additionally, it involved food offered to idols and fleeing idolatry (1 Corinthians Chapter 8). Therefore, Paul refers to the packaging of all these teachings as the traditions or ordinances he gave to them. Living holy and walking in righteousness is a tradition of the church. These were the tenets he wanted them to live by. However, it seems that these meaningful traditions are often neglected and replaced with the ones that serve the glory of man and are therefore of no effect.

Paul begins the chapter by referring to traditions because wearing a covering while praying or prophesying also represented a tradition or custom in Corinth. Therefore, he creates a parallel between two traditions; the traditions that he gave them and the one present at Corinth. Hence, before engaging in the tradition of men and women covering their heads, Paul makes it clear which traditions they are required to keep. On that account, the context for this entire dialogue on covering is <u>not</u> a commandment from Paul but a discussion on traditions between Paul and the church. On one hand, he gave them some traditions that they should keep. On the other hand, there was a tradition they needed clarification on and whether it applied to the church.

As mentioned, Corinth had an infusion of both Greek and

Roman culture and the covering of the head was a common practice or tradition in this cultural environment. Therefore, they wanted to incorporate this tradition into the church because it was established in this cultural setting. Consequently, from verses 4-10, Paul is essentially rehearsing the tradition in existence at Corinth during that time because the members wanted clarity on whether it applied to the church. Essentially, they were asking the proverbial question, "When in Rome should we do as the Romans do?" After the exchange, he then provides an answer on head covering. How do we know this? After outlining the tradition, Paul gives his input on the subject:

> But if any man seem to be contentious, <u>we have no such custom, neither the churches of God. (1 Corinthians 11:16)</u>

So after assessing the tradition on covering, Paul concluded that even though the custom existed at Corinth, the apostles had no such custom and it was not a custom or tradition to which the church was to be subjected. Instead, the focus was to follow the traditions he gave to them. The concentration should have been on traditions related to righteous living. Instead, it was on external traditions such as covering.

Hierarchy of Authority: Covering from God's Perspective

Notice that prior to addressing the subject of head covering, Paul, in a masterful fashion, approaches the topic by discussing covering from the aspect of the hierarchy of authority.

> But I would have you know, that the head of every man is Christ; and the head of the woman is the man; and the head of Christ is God. (1 Corinthians 11:3)

By offering this premise, he is saying to the church, "While you are concerned about a material covering, let me explain God's divine order for covering. While you are consumed with the matter of tradition and customs, let me explain divine covering from God's perspective. God's point of view always outweighs the traditions of men."

The word "head" in the context of 1 Corinthians Chapter 11, speaks of authority and denotes the position of a leader or ruler. However, "head," in the context of this passage, has to be understood <u>*within the boundaries of relationship and function*</u>. For example, Christ is the head or ruler of every man or believer (inclusive of women), which signifies His function in our relationship. Similarly, the head of the woman (wife) is not every man, in general. Rather, the head of the woman is distinctly her husband (Ephesians 5:21-23), which also speaks of his function in the relationship. We saw in the first chapter of this book how this was instituted in relation to Adam and his wife, Eve.

In its true sense, "head" is not simply a positional appointment, but it also refers to the mandate of responsibility. It surpasses the notion of simply being "in charge" and embraces the concept of servant leadership, which enriches the lives of others. Furthermore, in the context of a relationship, the passage says that the head of Christ is God. This denotes relationship and function in terms of the Father-Son relationship and their particular function in that relationship. Without question, the discussion of headship in this passage does not imply that one is less than or inferior to the other, but it primarily points to the specific function in the relationship. This is particularly evident in the examples that are offered. For instance, just as we cannot make the inference that Christ is inferior to God, for they are equal, we also cannot conclude that the woman is inferior to the man or her husband. The function is simply different.

Unfortunately, a misunderstanding of this passage, particularly as it pertains to men and women, has created a general perception that all men are superior to women and contributes to gender suppression. Additionally, let me say unequivocally that headship does not mean domination but speaks only of responsibility and function. To explain true covering, the context of the passage provides the hierarchy of authority for specific relationships.

In particular, if a woman is unmarried, Christ is also her covering. Moreover, the covering for a married woman is her husband, as well as Christ. Therefore, since Christ Himself serves as the covering for all women, a material covering is not a necessity. I reiterate that covering in relation to having a head doesn't mean to have someone as a subject, but it simply speaks of assuming responsibility. An example of this concerning a husband and wife is in the book of Ruth, where Ruth requested that Boaz spread his skirt over her. This act of covering was an indication that he would receive her and acknowledge her as a wife (Ruth 3:9). Hence, he would assume responsibility for her and redeem her. In a marriage relationship, the function of a husband is that of a head or "coverer." As believers, Christ is our coverer and Redeemer.

As mentioned, before reciting the custom on covering, which existed at the time in Corinth, Paul first establishes the framework on God's perspective of covering. Therefore, as the custom had a biased undertone, after stating the tradition, Paul levels the playing field between men and women in verses 11 and 12. This reference is from the Amplified Bible.

11. Nevertheless, woman is not independent of man, nor is man independent of woman.
12. For as the woman originates from the man, so also man is born through the woman; and all things [whether male or female] originate from God [as their creator]. (1 Corinthians 11:11-12)

In the midst of the discussion, these verses echo the sentiments of unity and equality between men and women. For outside the scope of the function in a marriage relationship, the distinction between men and women does not exist. Additionally, in true dialogue fashion, after a comprehensive conversation on the matter, Paul asks the Corinthian church, "Judge in yourselves: is it comely that a woman pray unto God uncovered?" In other words, Paul petitions the church to evaluate the tradition in light of God's Word and make a determination. Before offering the final word on the matter that covering the head while praying or prophesying is not a custom of the church (1 Corinthians 11:16), Paul adds that a woman's hair is also given to her as a covering.

In summary, instead of providing a concise answer regarding head covering, Paul, in response to their letter, uses the opportunity to reinforce what he communicated to them, as well as create a teachable moment. Therefore, after a lengthy exchange, which involved highlighting the traditions he gave the church in contrast to the ones at Corinth, he provides God's true perspective on covering. He concludes that head covering is not necessary.

So there you have it, Scripture does not require women to wear head coverings while praying or prophesying. Instead, the focus should be on keeping the traditions that pertain to holiness and righteousness, as well as those that foster unity in the church. As mentioned at the beginning of this chapter, as a woman, if you choose to wear a hat or a head covering while praying or prophesying, have comfort knowing that you do so based on your own volition, as an adornment, and from the position of liberty.

Weaker Vessel

In accordance with the principle that no passage of Scripture should be interpreted without consideration to "the whole of Scripture context," 1 Peter 3:1-7 also has to be assessed in light of this position. As a result of reading this passage in isolation or with prejudiced lenses, the church has made several inaccurate determinations resulting in gender biases against women. Furthermore, in examining this scripture, a broader spotlight is often placed on the portion pertaining to the function of the wife compared to that of the husband, thereby creating an imbalanced perspective.

1. Likewise, ye wives, be in subjection to your own husbands; that, if any obey not the word,

      they also may without the word be won by the conversation of the wives;
2. While they behold your chaste conversation coupled with fear.
3. Whose adorning let it not be that outward adorning of plaiting the hair, and of wearing of gold, or of putting on of apparel;
4. But let it be the hidden man of the heart, in that which is not corruptible, even the ornament of a meek and quiet spirit, which is in the sight of God of great price.
5. For after this manner in the old time the holy women also, who trusted in God, adorned themselves, being in subjection unto their own husbands:
6. Even as Sara obeyed Abraham, calling him lord: whose daughters ye are, as long as ye do well, and are not afraid with any amazement.
7. Likewise, ye husbands, dwell with them according to knowledge, giving honour unto the wife, as unto the weaker vessel, and as being heirs together of the grace of life; that your prayers be not hindered. (1 Peter 3:1-7)

First, in order to establish the correct parameter, it should be understood that the passage speaks specifically to a husband and wife relationship and not to men and women in general. Therefore, the offerings of the text are intended to foster an atmosphere of unity, godliness, and mutual respect within a marriage relationship. In that vein, the language used is designed to convey that message and not one of a disparaging nature.

Based on "the whole of Scripture context," the Bible is clear that the husband is the head of the wife and serves as her covering (1 Corinthians 11:3). In addition, it also admonishes the wife to submit to her husband as unto the Lord (Ephesians 5:22). Nevertheless, it is with the understanding that this exists within the atmosphere of mutual submission to one another in the fear of the Lord (Ephesians 5:21). Furthermore, it has already been determined that this relationship is not hinged on the notion that one is superior to the other, but it is simply based on God's order for the family. Additionally, it also highlights the responsibility and function of both the husband and the wife. Therefore, with the contribution of 1 Peter 3:1-7, the foundation is still the same. In fact, it is safe to surmise that the passage reinforces and echoes the same sentiments that were expressed earlier regarding a husband and wife relationship. It does this by adding perspective to the relationship and highlighting the responsibilities of both.

The wife is admonished to be in subjection to her <u>own</u> husband and demonstrate chaste behavior. If she has an unbelieving husband, he may be persuaded by her godly manner of life. Scripture refers to this expression of righteousness as an adornment or an ornament. The passage offers a comparison to emphasize that this decoration is based on the condition of the heart and not on external appearances. It makes a contrast by placing greater value on internal beauty rather than on external accessories. To be clear, the passage is not stating that women are prohibited from plaiting their hair, wearing gold, or putting on apparel (obviously). It is simply stating that compared to these external adornments, the ornament of a meek and quiet spirit is a greater price in the sight of God and benefits the marriage relationship.

As mentioned earlier, it seems that after discussing the responsibilities of the wife, the conversation falls off a cliff relative to the husband. However, in a corresponding fashion, husbands are encouraged to dwell with their wives according to knowledge. This means that a husband's relationship with his wife should be in accordance with what Scripture says. Along these lines, Ephesians 5:28-29 says,

28. So ought men to love their wives as their own bodies. He that loveth his wife loveth himself.
29. For no man ever yet hated his own flesh; but nourisheth and cherisheth it, even as the Lord the church

This also speaks of a husband being sensitive to both the physical and emotional needs of his wife.

Recently in the Bahamas, there was a growing debate on whether a husband could actually rape his wife. While this was a contentious discussion from various fractions, one thing is certain: if a husband follows the guidance of Scripture, such actions will not occur. Similarly, if the wife adheres to the same prescriptions, activities of this nature would not be a subject of marriage.

The husband is called to be thoughtful, considerate, and respectful to his wife, which is in harmony with the requirements of Ephesians 5:25-29. This also includes exercising patience, tenderness, and being delicate with respect to his wife. The passage summarizes this behavior as giving honor to his wife in recognition that she is the "weaker vessel."

Over the years, I have heard the term "weaker vessel" used in a pejorative manner as it pertains to women. First, Scripture does not say that the woman is weak. I am certain that it would not require an intense search to find women who possess abilities to the contrary. For women are indeed strong. However, in a comparative sense, the Bible uses the word "weaker" only to create a physical contrast between the vessel of a man and that of a woman. This, however, has no bearing on her spiritual or intellectual capabilities as an equal. Therefore, the phrase "weaker vessel" is actually a relative term.

This is why there are separate events for men and women when it comes to sporting competitions where physical abilities are a determining factor. This includes a myriad of activities such as basketball, track and field, tennis, boxing, and the like. However, for other events where physical abilities or strength are irrelevant, men and women strive for the mastery on equal footing. This could include activities such as chess, teaching, or other endeavors that require more intellect than physical ability. In regard to this earthy tabernacle, a man's body is generally physically stronger compared to that of a woman. Therefore, with the overarching responsibility of the husband being one of protection and care, he is admonished to respect his wife as the "weaker vessel." Hence, the comparison is more an admonition to the husband to be a protector and nourisher. These harmonize with his role as his wife's covering.

In providing a meaningful summary for this discussion, overall, the passage speaks of unity. It points out the responsibilities of both the husband and wife as they are heirs together of the grace of life. Additionally, it says that righteous behavior, mutual submission, and respect result in their prayers not being hindered or cut off.

Ministry Covering for Women

While having lunch with a few male friends, I asked the question, "Can a woman be a pastor?" Immediately, someone said no! In response, I asked, "why not?" The reply was, "I just don't think it's right!" I found it interesting that his conviction was not based on Scripture or any other reliable source, but simply on his feelings and personal opinion. To his credit, perhaps over time, fragments of teaching on the subject influenced him, but it was not sufficient to serve as a reliable source or reference. It is amazing how sometimes we can have strong convictions regarding a matter but no real foundation for it.

As the conversation progressed, someone else said, "Yes, a woman can be a pastor, but she has to be under a man." In other words, a man must serve as her covering.

Again, I asked the question, "why?" and not surprisingly, the response was similar to the first one. However, they also added, "Women are too emotional." Many times, when the question of women in a leadership role arises, whether it is in the church, government, or other institutions, as if by innate programming, this comment seems to be a default response, particularly by men and unfortunately, some women. Obviously, this statement is devoid of the fact that, as human beings, whether male or female, we all display a variety of emotions. For example, while there is a tendency for women to express more happiness or sadness, men tend to exhibit more anger. Nevertheless, our emotional expressions of the same feelings are sometimes different.

In many instances, the conclusion that women are too emotional is based on stereotypes, for those expressed by women are often more scrutinized than those displayed by men. Additionally, the condition of the world we live in today is predominantly a product of male leadership. History is a witness that it has not been without emotional upheaval. Certainly, if being too emotional was a disqualifier for leadership, then even in today's environment immediate recalls, especially in government are required. Nevertheless, one thing is clear, to complement each other, God made us different. However, even with our differences, He gave us both the common ability to have dominion and exercise authority.

Based on the interpretation of 1 Corinthians 11:3 that the man serves as the head or covering of the woman, the common perspective held by some is that this also pertains to her position and function in ministry. However, as we have determined, Scripture is abundantly clear that this covering speaks specifically to a husband and wife relationship and the husband's function and responsibility in the family.

Indeed, in a family setting, the husband is the head of the wife and serves as her covering. However, in a kingdom environment, which includes the church, the same principle does not apply. Being a male is not an inherent position of authority when it comes to the principles of God's kingdom. In fact, in Christ, male/female distinctions do not exist. Therefore, the context of 1 Corinthians 11:3 speaks of family conditions for covering and is not a general principle that a man has to be a covering for a woman in ministry. Nevertheless, as a good foundation for a family, mutual submission to each other and recognition of God's order for the family helps to foster an atmosphere of unity and equality regardless of the setting you are in.

For those who are opposed to or uncomfortable with women in ministry, in general, the appeasement seems to be that if a male is ultimately in charge, then this is acceptable. This subscribes to the notion that being a male is an automatic qualification for leadership and ministry. This is not supported by Scripture and is a totally gender-biased opinion. The common posture of those who see a woman functioning in ministry independent of a man is that she is either "usurping authority over the man," or that she has a "Jezebel spirit." In particular, the statement of usurping authority, which comes from 1 Timothy 1:12, is made without understanding what it means, or the circumstances in which it was said. The topic of usurping authority will be adequately addressed in Chapter 5.

Additionally, the term "Jezebel spirit," which is often used to categorize women as dominating and controlling, is also used with little regard for all the activities connected to Jezebel. Based on Scripture, Jezebel had Naboth killed in order to acquire his land for her husband, King Ahab (1 Kings 21). Additionally, she also had a relentless crusade for idol worship. She replaced the worship of God with the worship of Baal and ordered the annihilation of the prophets of God. Furthermore, Revelation 2:19-25 identifies Jezebel as a false prophet who promotes false teachings, seduction, fornication, idolatry, and fellowship with devils. Therefore, taken together, the "Jezebel spirit" is generally characterized by idolatry, heresy, and immoral behavior. On that point, such attributes are not limited to women only, for the Scripture attaches them to men as well. The "Jezebel spirit" is not gender-specific; the focus is on behavior. It has nothing to do with a woman who functions in ministry independent of a man or who is perceived as aggressive. It is a quality that is in opposition to God, promotes false teaching, and subscribes to the works of the flesh.

The Progressive Nature of the New Testament

Those who oppose the appointment of women in ministry make the argument that even in the New Testament, the leadership appointments consisted primarily of men. To support their position, they highlight that even Jesus during His earthly ministry specifically appointed twelve male apostles. Moreover, to further justify their conviction, the point is also made that in Acts 6:1-7, the seven who were chosen by the apostles to distribute goods to the poor were also men. Therefore, the question is asked, if women could function in ministry, why weren't they chosen in these instances?

In addressing this perspective, it has to be understood that just like the Old Testament, the New Testament follows a progressive pattern in terms of its writing. First, during Jesus' earthly ministry, He was still functioning under the dispensation of the Law. Galatians 4:7 says, "But when the fulness of the time was come, God sent forth his Son, made of a woman, made under the law." In fact, the dispensation of grace wasn't ushered in until the death and resurrection of Jesus Christ. Therefore, although the Gospels are contained in the New Testament, the customs and principles of the Law were still in effect.

In terms of their primary function in the New Testament, the four Gospels represent a transition from the dispensation of Law to the dispensation of grace. One aspect of this can be seen in what is commonly referred to as "The Sermon on the Mount." In promoting the transition, Jesus, in Matthew Chapters 5 through 7 uses the contrasting phrases, "You have heard," followed by, "But I say unto you." By these statements, He was creating a distinction between the acceptable practices under the Law, compared to those of the kingdom of God. In essence, He was introducing a new culture, one that is based on the principles of God's kingdom.

Among many things, the Bible is also a cultural book and the progression from the Old Testament to the New Testament represents a change in cultural norms. However, even though the kingdom's cultural principles were gradually being introduced, appointments were still based on the premise of the Law and the existing cultural environment. Therefore, when Jesus appointed His twelve apostles, He appointed men as it was still a male-dominated society and under the Law.

Furthermore, when we examine the book of Acts, the progressive format of the New Testament is also evident. With the church being recently established, many of the cultural changes of the dispensation of grace had not yet taken effect. In fact, some were unknown. Hence, the changes were not automatically reflected in the operation and functioning of the church. The cultural norms of the Old Testament were comprehensive in that they included certain religious, social, ethnic, and gender values, etc. Plus, knowledge of changes to these norms was gradually being revealed. For example, despite the ethnic and social changes in relation to the position of the Gentiles, this was initially unknown to the church. However, in Acts Chapter 10, based on the vision Peter received from the Lord, this change was revealed to him. Related to the details of the vision, Peter says in Acts 10:34-35, "Of a truth I perceive that God is no respecter of persons: But in every nation he that feareth him, and worketh righteousness, is accepted with him." Hence, despite the Gentiles being included in salvation, up to this point, the focus was only on the Jews. Consequently, when the leaders of the church heard that Peter had fellowshipped with Gentiles, they contended with him. Again, the reason they disputed with him was because the prevailing culture along with the Law forbade the association of Jews and Gentiles. However, in Acts Chapter 11 after Peter rehearsed the details of the vision to the leadership of the church, they glorified God, and the Gentiles were accepted. Before this revelation, Gentiles were not appointed to leadership positions in the church despite the allowance based on grace.

The apostle Paul provides further insight into the unity of Jews and Gentiles in one body in his letter to the Ephesians. However, as mentioned, during the initial stages of the church, this truth was unknown. Similar examples of this scenario are evident concerning the religious practice of circumcision in Acts Chapter 15 and the baptism of the Holy Ghost in Acts Chapter 19.

I reiterate that changes relative to the dispensation of grace and the principles of the kingdom of God were systematically being revealed to the church during its early years. All the changes that the church today is aware of were not known at the inception of the church. Hence, the appointments and functioning of the church reflected what was known at particular junctures. Another example of this was also evident in the dynamics that existed between men and women. Even though Galatians 3:28 says, "There is neither Jew nor Greek, there is neither bond nor free, there is neither male nor female: for ye are all one in Christ Jesus," the initial ministerial appointments of the church did not reflect this change. Again, this is because this truth was unknown to the church at that time. Therefore, in Acts 6:1-7, when the apostles appointed the seven men to oversee the distribution of goods to the poor, the appointments were not based on Galatians 3:28. In fact, the epistle was not even written at the time. In truth, in terms of revelation knowledge, the church, during this period, was a work-in-progress. However, later in Romans Chapter 16, there is evidence of the effects of the change taking root, particularly as it relates to women.

In the closing remarks of Paul's letter to the Romans, he says in Romans 16:1-2:

1. I commend unto you Phebe our sister, which is a servant of the church which is at Cenchrea:
2. That ye receive her in the Lord, as becometh saints, and that ye assist her in whatsoever business she hath need of you: for she hath been a succourer of many, and of myself also.

The word "servant" in Romans 16:1 is the Greek word *diakonos* from which we get the English word "deacon." Hence, she is noted as a deacon or deaconess and the qualifications of a deacon can be aptly attributed to her. Additionally, in the same chapter, Paul also highlights Priscilla and her husband Aquila.

3. Greet Priscilla and Aquila my helpers in Christ Jesus:
4. Who have for my life laid down their own necks: unto whom not only I give thanks, but also all the churches of the Gentiles.
5. Likewise greet the church that is in their house. (Romans 16:3-5)

Without elaborating on the fact that Paul mentioned her name first, notice that he specifically refers to them as his helpers in Christ. The word "helper" is the Greek word *synergos,* and it also means fellowlabourer. In other words, they were engaged in the same work in relation to the gospel. In 1 Corinthians 3:9, Paul uses the same word "fellowlabourer" in describing the work and relationship between him and Apollos.

As it pertains to the work of the gospel he says, "I have planted, Apollos watered, but God gave the increase." From the context of the passage, Paul communicates the significance of Apollos' work when he concludes they were labourers together with God. Hence, the acknowledgement of Priscilla and Aquila using the same reference is a significant commendation. Also, Romans 16:5 speaks to the church that is in their house. Priscilla will be further discussed in Chapter 6 of this book.

Throughout the remainder of Romans Chapter 16, Paul commends several other women, complimenting them for their work and holding them in high esteem. For example:

Salute Andronicus and Junia, my kinsmen, and my fellowprisoners, who are of note among the

> apostles, who also were in Christ before me. (Romans 16:7)

> Salute Tryphena and Tryphosa, who labour in the Lord. Salute the beloved Persis, which laboured much in the Lord. (Romans 16:12)

Paul's remarks in this chapter certainly do not convey the message that women should be silent in the church or that it is a shame for women to speak in the church. On the contrary, the references illustrate women who were engaged in the work of the ministry on multiple levels.

From the inception of the church in Acts Chapter 2 to the time Paul makes these statements in the book of Romans, certainly, the landscape has changed concerning the direct involvement of women in ministry. Hence, from a scriptural perspective, we see an increase in their involvement over this time. This is a manifestation of the progressive nature of the New Testament, as a result of the church coming into the knowledge that in Christ, male and female distinctions no longer exist.

Once this truth became known it was then reflected in the functioning and operation of the church. Additionally, because this change represented a significant change in the cultural environment that existed, its adoption did not occur overnight. In fact, as evident by the current position of many in the church, the change still has not been fully embraced.

In summary, when we read the New Testament, we have to be cognizant that the church was evolving, and the changes were gradually being implemented based on what was made known.

The Qualifications for Office

As I stated before, the atmosphere in which the New Testament was written was also a culture influenced by male dominance. Therefore, despite eliminating the distinctions between males and females in Christ, many aspects of the writings still reflected the cultural environment that existed. Hence, the pronouns used were predominately male-oriented. However, in examining the writings, we have to appreciate that many of them are not gender-specific but apply to both men and women. Additionally, even in some cases where the qualifications for the offices are listed, they are based on the principle of being a male.

For example, in 1 Timothy 3:1-13, the qualifications of a bishop and deacon seem to suggest that it is an office primarily for men, especially with the inclusion of marriage and household management. Titus 1:5-9 offers the same implication regarding an elder. As a point of reference, the positions of elder, pastor, and bishop are identical offices according to Scripture with no distinction between the three. For a comprehensive discussion on that point, please see my book, *The Five-Fold Ministry Gifts: Understanding the Gifts of Christ in Light of God's Purpose.*

For this discussion on the offices of a bishop and deacon, we will focus on 1 Timothy Chapter 3.

The Qualifications of a Bishop

1. This is a true saying, If a man desire the office of a bishop, he desireth a good work.

2. A bishop then must be blameless, the husband of one wife, vigilant, sober, of good behaviour, given to hospitality, apt to teach;
3. Not given to wine, no striker, not greedy of filthy lucre; but patient, not a brawler, not covetous;
4. One that ruleth well his own house, having his children in subjection with all gravity;
5. (For if a man know not how to rule his own house, how shall he take care of the church of God?)
6. Not a novice, lest being lifted up with pride he fall into the condemnation of the devil.
7. Moreover he must have a good report of them which are without; lest he fall into reproach and the snare of the devil. (1 Timothy 3:1-7)

The Qualifications of a Deacon

8. Likewise must the deacons be grave, not doubletongued, not given to much wine, not greedy of filthy lucre;
9. Holding the mystery of the faith in a pure conscience.
10. And let these also first be proved; then let them use the office of a deacon, being found blameless.
11. Even so must their wives be grave, not slanderers, sober, faithful in all things.

12. Let the deacons be the husbands of one wife, ruling their children and their own houses well.
13. For they that have used the office of a deacon well purchase to themselves a good degree, and great boldness in the faith which is in Christ Jesus. (1 Timothy 3:8-13)

On the surface, the passages would seem to imply that the offices of a bishop and deacon are specifically intended for men. Those who hold this persuasion point out that the pronouns used and the accompanying qualifications are distinctly male-oriented. However, as we have concluded, Scripture was written in a culture of male dominance and the writings reflect that influence. For example, to reiterate this point, Galatians 6:1 says, "Brethren, if a man be overtaken in a fault, ye which are spiritual, restore such an one in the spirit of meekness; considering thyself, lest thou also be tempted." Based on the pronoun used in this verse, are we also to infer that only men are capable of falling into sin?

In 1 Timothy 3:1, the word "man" is translated as "anyone" or "whoever." Hence, though it may seem predisposed to one gender, it is a generic term for all humanity, which includes both male and female. For instance, Genesis 1:27 says, "So God created man in his own image, in the image of God created he him; male and female created he them." Moreover, with the word "man" being used in 1 Timothy Chapter 3, it is only reasonable that the qualifications would also be male-oriented. The requirements simply reflect the nature of the pronoun being used.

Based on this premise, 1 Timothy Chapter 3 says both the

bishop and the deacon must be "the husband of one wife" and have the ability to "rule his own house well." Titus Chapter 1 also presents the same requirements concerning an elder. First, are these passages implying that marriage is a prerequisite for the positions? Of course not! By no means is the apostle Paul conveying that to assume leadership responsibility in the church, the requirement is marriage. For he himself was unmarried. On the contrary, this statement is based on the condition that the bishop/elder or deacon is already married. Hence, the main point being emphasized is that if the candidate is married, he must be monogamous and consequently faithful to his wife.

In a culture where polygamy was practiced, Scripture highlights that the requirement of the offices and of the church is one of monogamy. A bishop/elder or deacon must only have one wife. He must be "a one-woman man." The offices require being faithful to your spouse. To that I add, staying married and not being devoted or faithful does not constitute the "one-wife" obligation. Additionally, the suggestion that a man who has been divorced cannot qualify for these positions is not the context of the passages.

Moreover, to add more context to the statement regarding marriage, we need to reconcile it with 1 Corinthians Chapter 7. Recall that in that chapter, Paul provides insight concerning marriage in relation to doing the work of the Lord. 1 Corinthians 7:32-33 says, "He that is married cares for the things of the world, how he may please his wife; however, he that is unmarried cares for the things of the Lord, how he may please the Lord." Therefore, Paul, in advocating that believers remain unmarried says it allows them to attend to the work of the Lord without distraction.

Furthermore, he says in 1 Corinthians 7:7 he wishes everyone was unmarried like him. However, he also understands that not everyone has the gift of celibacy; therefore, marriage is a necessity.

When we reconcile 1 Corinthians Chapter 7 with 1 Timothy Chapter 3, it is apparent Scripture is not insisting that marriage is a precondition for the work of the Lord. On the contrary, the communication is that in the state of marriage, the righteous requirement is monogamy and faithfulness. In summary, the statement regarding being the husband of one wife is more aligned to righteous living than gender or marital status. In fact, when we take into account all the qualifications for ministry leadership mentioned in the chapter, the focus is really on walking in righteousness.

1 Timothy Chapter 3 also speaks of bishops/elders and deacons ruling their own houses well and having children not accused of being unruly. As before, this is based on the condition that they are married and have children; therefore, they have a household. This is a qualification that involves authority and responsibility. Again, with the writings of Scripture being predominately male-oriented, this qualification is also masculine in nature. Hence, a man with a wife is expected to function as the head of his family and exercise responsibility.

On that note, 1 Timothy 3:5 says plainly, "For if a man know not how to rule his own house, how shall he take care of the church of God?" Therefore, as the steward of God or the manager of God's household, the requirement of the office would be for the person to properly govern his/her own house. For clarification, the reference to children in 1 Timothy 3:4 does not apply to adult children but rather, to those who are underage. Therefore, they must not be disobedient to authority, disorderly, or lawless. Hence, in governing his/her house, the children of that house must be in submission and he/she should exercise seriousness in this regard.

Additionally, based on the designation of deacon that was attributed to Phebe in Romans 16:1, it is clear that the office is not reserved specifically for men. Also, this further supports the fact that the qualifications mentioned for the office simply reflect a male-dominated environment.

Ministry Gifts

The same principle we discussed in 1 Timothy Chapter 3 is also evident in Ephesians Chapter 4. This is another example of the male-oriented nature of the Scriptures concerning church leadership. Ephesians 4:8 says, "When he (Christ) ascended up on high, he led captivity captive, and gave gifts unto men." At face-value, this would also give the impression that ministry gifts or the gifts of Christ only pertain to men. However, the word "men" in this passage is also a generic term for all humanity, meaning both men and women. It is the Greek word *anthropos*, from which we get the word "anthropology."

According to *Webster's Dictionary*, anthropology is the science of human beings. It studies people, especially their history, development, distribution, biological characteristics, and culture. Hence, the gifts that Christ gave are given to all humanity, which includes both men and women. What specifically are these gifts?

> And he gave some, apostles; and some, prophets; and some, evangelists; and some, pastors and teachers. (Ephesians 4:11)

Furthermore, these ministry gifts are for a distinct purpose as outlined in Ephesians 4:12:

- For the perfecting of the saints
- For the work of the ministry
- For the edifying of the body of Christ

Therefore, women can also be apostles, prophets, evangelists, pastors, and teachers as the gifts of Christ are not male-oriented. Isn't it ironic that even in its acceptance of women functioning in the five-fold ministry gifts, the church is more accepting of a woman being an evangelist or prophet/prophetess as opposed to her being an apostle, pastor, or teacher? However, as mentioned, these ministry gifts are not gender-specific. Additionally, Ephesians 4:16 says that when there is an effectual working by every member of the body and every joint supplies its part, then the body grows and edifies itself in love. Again, for more on the five-fold ministry gifts, please see my book, *The Five-Fold Ministry Gifts: Understanding the Gifts of Christ in Light of God's Purpose.*

Based on the sum total of our study to this point, it can be comfortably concluded that the perspective a woman should not hold an office in the church does not stand the test of "the whole of Scripture context." Is it practical to accept that in Christ there is neither male nor female, but when it comes to ministry and offices related to Christ, there is a distinction? 1 Corinthians Chapter 12, while underscoring unity and equality in the body of Christ, emphasizes that the body grows based on the contribution of every member. As stated, any house divided against itself cannot stand or experience the growth for which it has been ordained.

WOMEN TEACHING AND USURPING AUTHORITY OVER THE MAN

The Context of Ephesians and 1 Timothy

Another popular passage of Scripture used to disprove women speaking in the church or functioning in a leadership capacity in the church is 1 Timothy 2:11-12.

> 11. Let the woman learn in silence with all subjection.
> 12. But I suffer not a woman to teach, nor to usurp authority over the man, but to be in silence.

Just like 1 Corinthians 14:34-35, the assessment of this passage appears to suggest that when it comes to the church, women are not to teach or be in positions of authority over men. Instead, they ought to be silent. If that were the case, it would seem to contradict everything we have determined up to this point. In fact, it also seems to disavow the conclusion of unity and equality in the household of faith. However, just as we have done throughout the course of this study, let us allow the Bible to interpret itself or, simply put, let Scripture interpret Scripture. What message is this scripture expressing in terms of the relationship between men and women?

By this point, it should be apparent that the setting in which a scripture exists is of paramount importance as it contributes to its correct perspective and meaning. In that regard, it should be noted that after establishing the church at Ephesus, Paul left Timothy there and sent him letters with instructions on how to deal with the false teachers and other matters of the church. *Hence, the epistles of 1 and 2 Timothy pertain to the conditions that existed at the church at Ephesus.*

> As I besought thee to abide still at Ephesus, when I went into Macedonia, that thou mightest charge some that they teach no other doctrine. (1 Timothy 1:3)

As these two epistles have a direct relationship with the conditions that existed in Ephesus at the time, there is a correlation between the context of the book of Ephesians and the context of the epistles to Timothy. Therefore, 1 Timothy is better appreciated by using the book of Ephesians as a backdrop. The questions must be asked, what is the general context of Ephesians, and what is its specific communication regarding men and women?

As I stated earlier, the prevailing theme of the book of Ephesians is that of unity and equality. Recall that it speaks of removing walls that separate humanity, thereby creating one new man in Christ. It talks about citizens who are members of one household or one family (Ephesians 2:13-18). In addition, Ephesians 4:4-6 makes a resounding contribution to the theme of unity and equality by saying:

4. There is one body, and one Spirit, even as ye are called in one hope of your calling;
5. One Lord, one faith, one baptism,
6. One God and Father of all, who is above all, and through all, and in you all.

Moreover, Ephesians Chapter 5 speaks of what fosters an atmosphere of unity and equality in a marriage setting. Therefore, with this as a foundation, the message to Timothy at Ephesus would not contradict this, as it is written to the same audience. I ask you; would Paul send one message regarding men and women to the Ephesian church in the book of Ephesians and send a contrasting message to the same people in the book of 1 Timothy? Furthermore, the communication offered in Ephesians Chapter 5 regarding men and women occurs within the context of marriage. However, even within this atmosphere, the message of unity and equality persists despite differing roles.

Different functions, therefore, do not diminish the essence of unity and equality. Hence, Ephesians 5:21 begins the discussion with the general communication, "submitting yourselves one to another in the fear of God."

Within this environment of unity and mutual submission, there are specific functions and responsibilities for the husband and wife for unity and equality to persist. The husband is the head or the covering of his wife and the wife is to submit to her own husband as unto the Lord.

The husband is also admonished to love his wife and give himself for her. He is to follow the example of Christ, though it may not be required to the same degree of death as the passage states. Moreover, the husband's role is to bring his wife into a position of glory, splendor, or excellence. This is accomplished by loving his wife as he loves himself. As a covering for his wife, the husband serves as a nourisher and one who cherishes her. This is what 1 Peter 3:7 refers to as giving honor to the wife. The responsibility of the wife is to reverence or obey her husband. Furthermore, the relationship of a husband and his wife serves as an earthy practical illustration of the relationship between Christ and the church. Therefore, the principles that exist with Christ and the church should also be present in a marriage relationship.

Nowhere in this exchange on marriage is the suggestion that the woman is inferior to her husband or that he dominates her. Hence, the conversation of the dynamics between a man and woman discussed in the book of 1 Timothy cannot be appreciated without embracing the context of the book of Ephesians. I reiterate, 1 Timothy 2:11-12 has to be read through the lens of Ephesians Chapter 5.

The next point to take into account relative to the context of the book of 1 Timothy, is that this epistle, as well as the book of

1 Corinthians, were both written by the apostle Paul. Therefore, based on the perspective concerning women in 1 Corinthians Chapter 11 and 1 Corinthians Chapter 14, the same tenets also apply to the book of 1 Timothy. Is it rational that Paul would give credence to women praying and prophesying (which includes teaching) in the church at Corinth, only to renege on this position and inform the church at Ephesus that women are to be silent and not teach? It was already established that, on occasion, the epistles were exchanged between churches. Could you imagine if the communication to one church regarding a matter was totally different from the instruction to another church concerning the same subject? Certainly, this is not the case.

As we will conclude, the contexts of the books of 1 Timothy and Ephesians do not contradict each other but are in perfect agreement.

In unison, the perspective of the Scriptures is consistent with the fact that as it pertains to men and women in the kingdom of God, there are no differences based on gender. The only distinction that exists between men and women according to Scripture involves their function and responsibility in a marriage relationship where the man is the head of the woman or her covering. In this regard, the context of 1 Timothy Chapter 2 takes place within the same parameters of marriage as discussed in 1 Corinthians Chapter 11 and Ephesians Chapter 5.

8. I will therefore than men pray everywhere, lifting up holy hands, without wrath and doubting.
9. In like manner also, that women adorn themselves in modest apparel, with shamefacedness

and sobriety; not with braided hair, or gold, or pearls, or costly array;

10. But (which becometh women professing godliness) with good works.
11. Let the woman learn in silence with all subjection.
12. But I suffer not a woman to teach, nor to usurp authority over the man, but to be in silence.
13. For Adam was first formed, then Eve.
14. And Adam was not deceived, but the woman being deceived was in the transgression. (1 Timothy 2:8-14)

After 1 Timothy 2:8-10 states acceptable practices for both men and women, in general, the focus then shifts to a woman in the context of a marriage for the remainder of the chapter. Therefore, the conversation is specific to a married woman and her husband. The Greek word for woman in 1 Timothy 2:11-12 is *gyne*. It refers to a wife and the context of the passage supports this. Furthermore, the Greek word for man in 1 Timothy 2:12 is *aner*. It refers to a husband and is also supported by the context of the passage.

Let the Woman Learn in Silence

When 1 Timothy 2:11 says, "Let the woman learn in silence with all subjection," what is the message being conveyed here? Recall that one of the constituents of the context of Scripture is "whole of Scripture context," which means that the perspective of a particular subject must be able to stand the test of the whole of Scripture. When compared to the conclusion of other scriptures, does the common perspective of a woman "learning in silence" in the church hold up or does it contradict other scriptures pertaining to the topic?

1 Timothy Chapter 2 has to be viewed in the context of the other scriptures that speak on the subject. By doing this, passages of Scripture are not interpreted in isolation or apart from the whole of Scripture. Based on our study to this point, certainly, the notion that a woman is to sit and be quiet in the church or in any environment does not hold up when compared to other scriptures or the whole of Scripture. Remember the response the apostle Paul provided in 1 Corinthians 15:36 regarding women being silent in the church. To that notion, he offered a resounding "What?!"

In what setting and in what context does 1 Timothy 2:11 admonish a woman to "learn in silence with all subjection?" Recall that 1 Corinthians Chapter 11 identifies the man (husband) as being the head or the covering for the woman (wife). However, this still does not convey the message of dominance or that she is inferior. Therefore, 1 Timothy Chapter 2 in supporting this concept speaks of a family setting and the proper order within the family. As the husband is the head of the wife, 1 Timothy 2:11 is not suggesting that the woman simply sits and be quiet. Rather, it admonishes her that while increasing her knowledge of the Scriptures or any other discipline, she should still respect her husband's position. This is the same message of subjection that Ephesians 5:22-24 speaks of. Hence, the two passages are in harmony with each other.

22. Wives, submit yourselves unto your own husbands, as unto the Lord.
23. For the husband is the head of the wife, even as Christ is the head of the church: and he is the saviour of the body.
24. Therefore as the church is subject unto Christ, so let the wives be to their own husbands in every thing. (Ephesians 5:22-24)

1 Timothy 2:11 is a statement that speaks of the disposition of a wife in relation to her husband with the acknowledgment that he is the head of the family.

Teaching and Usurping Authority Over the Man

As the setting for 1 Timothy 2:12 is within the confines of a marriage, then the instruction regarding teaching and usurping authority also relates to a marriage relationship or a family and has no direct bearing on church function. Just like the previous point, the question has to be asked, does the perspective that a woman should not teach (in the church) stand the test of the whole of Scripture? Obviously, based on the perspective of 1 Corinthians 11 and 14, women have the endorsement of Scripture to both prophesy and teach in the church. Therefore, "teach" refers to a particular context as it pertains to a marriage environment. What does 1 Timothy 2:12 mean when it says, "But I suffer not a woman to teach, not to usurp authority over the man, but to be in silence"?

In general, teach means to impart instruction or instill doctrine. Furthermore, the word "usurp" means to exercise authority over someone. It specifically means to seize and hold the power of another by force without legal authority. The Bible gives legal authority to the man as the head of his wife and family. Therefore, within the confines of a marriage relationship or family, as the man is the head of the wife and her covering, she is admonished not to continuously instruct her husband or undermine his position or authority in the family.

Most men would tell you that the pain they feel when they are undermined by their wives is sometimes worse than any physical pain that can be inflicted upon them. Hence, through husband and wife interaction, the wife is called upon not to constantly impart knowledge to her husband in an instructing manner or as though she is teaching him. This ties in with the context of verse 11 that even though the wife may know more, she should still be in subjection to her husband and respect his position. Moreover, the fact that she may know more does not give her the right to usurp authority over her husband or seize his authority in the family.

Statements by women such as "I wear the pants in this house," which figuratively speaks of authority, can be an example of the appearance of usurping authority. Expressions of this nature are what 1 Timothy 2:12 refers to as usurping authority over the man who is the head or covering of his wife. This perspective is consistent in both Ephesians Chapter 5 and 1 Corinthians Chapter 11.

As you may be aware, there are often extremes in everything. Just how the implication here is not for a wife to sit in silence, this also does not mean that the husband has all the answers and should not listen to the suggestions of his wife. Ephesians 5:21 sets the stage that a husband and wife are to be in subjection to each other in the fear of the Lord. This creates an atmosphere of unity and equality in the marriage, even though the man is the head of the family. For example, even in a work setting, despite the manager being the head (in this instance a male), there are certain areas in which he has to depend on or submit to the expertise of others (perhaps females). Does this mean that his authority is being usurped or undermined? Of course not! Also, does this infer that unity does not exist? In fact, this bolsters unity and the spirit of equality within the organization.

Similarly, in a family, there may be areas in which the wife is more proficient and knowledgeable. In such circumstances, it would behoove the husband to submit to her expertise in these matters. This creates unity and equality in the family. On the contrary, not taking this approach could be to the detriment of the family. Certainly, the admonition of Ephesians 5:21 is a wonderful approach in addressing any challenges that may arise, particularly in the family.

Keep in mind that the underlying function of a woman in a marriage relationship is to be a help meet. As we have determined, this is one who has the power and ability to help. It also speaks of one who has the power to surround. Undertaking this role is possible even with the husband serving as her covering.

A true perspective of the Scriptures makes it clear that there is a distinction between a woman's function in the church and her function in a marriage relationship or family. In Christ, women are equal to men and their husbands in relation to the kingdom of God. However, in a marriage, the husband is the head of the wife and serves as her covering. Therefore, the circumstances of 1 Timothy 2:11-12 points to a marriage relationship and not conditions of the church.

Furthermore, with an understanding of what it means to usurp authority, a woman who is a pastor and functions independently of a man is not usurping authority over a man. The authority as the head is given to a man (husband) within the confines of a family. Such authority in the kingdom of God or the church bestowed solely to the man does not exist. Therefore, it is impossible to usurp or seize authority that was not granted in the first place. In Christ, male and female distinctions do not exist. Moreover, Acts 10:34-35 provides a principle and says, "Of a truth, God is not a respecter of persons, but those who fear Him and work righteousness are accepted with Him."

God's Original Order

To appreciate the context of 1 Timothy Chapter 2, the question should be asked, in what scenario was the man given authority over the woman? Based on the principle that Scripture interprets Scripture, the answer is provided in the remaining verses of the chapter. In qualifying the context for usurping authority, 1 Timothy 2:13 brings Adam and Eve, the first family, into the discussion.

> For Adam was first formed, then Eve. (1 Timothy 2:13)

With this inclusion, it conveys the message that the context of teaching and usurping authority pertains to a husband and wife in a family setting. Moreover, the order of creation mentioned here has its foundation in the book of Genesis. In that vein, the principle being employed here is called "the first mention principle."

This principle states that in order to get the fundamental meaning of what is being said, you have to go to the place in Scripture where it was first mentioned. The order of creation relative to male and female is recorded in Genesis Chapter 2.

18. And the LORD God said, It is not good that the man should be alone; I will make him an help meet for him.
19. And out of the ground the LORD God formed every beast of the field, and every fowl of the air; and brought them unto Adam to see what he would call them: and whatsoever Adam called every living creature, that was the name thereof.
20. And Adam gave names to all cattle, and to the fowl of the air, and to every beast of the field; but for Adam there was not found an help meet for him.
21. And the LORD God caused a deep sleep to fall upon Adam, and he slept: and he took one of his ribs, and closed up the flesh instead thereof;
22. And the rib, which the LORD God had taken from man, made he a woman, and brought her unto the man.
23. And Adam said, This is now bone of my bones, and flesh of my flesh: she shall be called Woman, because she was taken out of Man.

24. Therefore shall a man leave his father and his mother, and shall cleave unto his wife: and they shall be one flesh. (Genesis 2:18-24)

The above passage therefore supports the position that Adam was first formed and then Eve. However, according to 1 Timothy 2:14 and Genesis 3:16, this was not the basis for the man being placed as the head of the family.

1 Timothy 2:14 says, "And Adam was not deceived, but the woman being deceived was in the transgression." In explaining how the husband became the head of the wife, the verse refers to the judgment that was imposed on the woman in Genesis 3. As a result of the transgression, Genesis 3:16 says, "Thy desire shall be to thy husband, and he shall rule over thee." Hence, included in the individual judgments for the woman, was that she would now be in subjection to her husband. Therefore, as it pertains to a family setting, the husband became the head of the wife. This speaks of his position of authority in the family.

It is within this framework that 1 Timothy 2:12 admonishes the wife not to usurp or seize the authority of her husband. Moreover, because the woman was deceived or tricked by the serpent, the penalty also involved her ability to instruct or offer guidance to her husband. 1 Timothy 2:12 refers to this as teaching. This passage has nothing to do with a woman's role or function in the church but specifically refers to a marriage relationship. Therefore, since the man is the head of the family, the wife should not continuously instruct him or usurp his authority in the family.

As I mentioned in Chapter 1, when we examine the first three chapters of the book of Genesis, there are two distinct conditions in operation. There is a kingdom environment and there is also a marriage or family setting. First, when God created humanity, He did so in a kingdom environment. In this kingdom atmosphere, God gave both man and woman dominion.

> 26. And God said, Let us make man in our image, after our likeness: and let them have dominion over the fish of the sea, and over the fowl of the air, and over the cattle, and over all the earth, and over every creeping thing that creepeth upon the earth.
> 27. So God created man in his own image, in the image of God created he him; male and female created he them. (Genesis 1:26-27)

In Chapter 1, we also discussed that the word "dominion" is a kingdom word, which signifies that Adam and Eve existed in a kingdom setting. Adam and Eve, though on Earth, were representatives of the kingdom of heaven. Prior to sin, there was unity and equality between males and females in a kingdom environment. As far as the kingdom of God is concerned, Adam and Eve were both given dominion and there was no distinction based on gender. This was the original order before sin. However, when Adam and Eve sinned, God's kingdom rule on Earth was interrupted and replaced by another dominion. Colossians 1:13 refers to this dominion as the power or kingdom of darkness.

When Jesus came and declared that the kingdom of heaven was at hand in Matthew 4:17, this represented the reintroduction of the kingdom of God on Earth. Inherent in this was the reestablishment of the kingdom principles, which existed from the beginning. This includes the equality of men and women. Hence, Galatians 3:28 says that in Christ there is neither male nor female for we are one in Christ.

In addition to the kingdom setting mentioned in Genesis, there was also a family setting. It is in this circumstance that the order of creation mentioned in 1 Timothy 2:13 is relevant. Because of sin and judgment, the original conditions changed. Genesis Chapter 3 provides the account of the Devil tempting Eve who consequently ate from the tree of the knowledge of good and evil. Thereafter, she gave the fruit to Adam and he also ate (Genesis 3:1-7). Based on this circumstance, 1 Timothy 2:14 says, "And Adam was not deceived, but the woman being deceived was in the transgression." Therefore, included in the judgment of the transgression was that a man's wife would now be in subjection to her husband. This condition relative to the family persists despite the redemptive work of Christ and the reestablishment of the kingdom of God. Again, as it applies to men and women, we have to make the distinction between what pertains to a kingdom environment or the church and what applies to a family setting.

Based on the reconciliation of Scripture, the Bible is abundantly clear that in a kingdom environment, gender identification is non-existent. It is important that in terms of context and perspective of Scripture that we do not confuse a kingdom setting with a family setting. In the next chapter, we will continue the discussion on male and female identity in the kingdom of God.

Perhaps it is worth reinforcing that as the relationship between a husband and his wife is one of unity and equality, this persists even within the church out of respect for one another. In the spirit of mutual submission to each other and recognition of her husband as the head, despite their function in the church, this should not erode this principle.

ONE IN CHRIST

Gender Identity in Christ

> 27. For as many of you as have been baptized into Christ have put on Christ.
> 28. There is neither Jew nor Greek, there is neither bond nor free, there is neither male nor female: for ye are all one in Christ Jesus. (Galatians 3:27-28)

With all intention, I did not begin the discussion of women in ministry with Galatians 3:27-28 or place significant attention to it until now. Often, in soliciting feedback on the veracity of women in ministry, this is one of the first scriptures used to sanction the position. As in the case of using notable women in Scripture as a validation, this passage is also a common starting point. Certainly, of all the scriptures, this one offers the clearest and most concise position on unity and equality between men and women in the kingdom of God. It is the preverbal straight-line answer, and its perspective is unmistakable. Having reconciled the other scriptures that are commonly used to limit or dismiss the role of women in ministry, the inclusion of this passage is the prominent icing on the cake.

Based on everything discussed to this point, it is obvious that in the kingdom of God, gender identity does not exist. Only in a marriage environment is there a distinction between male and female and even this is not one of oppression but rather mutual submission and love.

Clothed in Christ

According to Galatians 3:27-28, when we are baptized or immersed into Christ, we "put on Christ." Therefore, what you put on identifies who you are and allows you to conform to that image. When we see someone in a particular uniform, the emphasis is not who he or she is as an individual, but rather what the uniform represents. For example, police officers in uniform depict protection, authority, order, safety, law, etc., and they function on behalf of the administration or governing authority that appointed them. Furthermore, the administration has conferred equal authority to everyone wearing the uniform, and personality or gender is a nonfactor. So, when we put on Christ, the authority of everyone clothed in Christ is also equal. When the Father looks at us, He does not see who we were; He sees whom we are clothed with. He sees Christ. If we have any other perspective, we are seeing each other based on our fleshly identification.

16. Wherefore henceforth know we no man after the flesh: yea, though we have known Christ after the flesh, yet now henceforth know we him no more.
17. Therefore if any man be in Christ, he is a new creature: old things are passed away; behold, all things are become new. (2 Corinthians 5:16-17)

The term, "know we no man after the flesh," speaks to recognizing, evaluating, and even accepting each other based on the fleshly tabernacle that we are clothed in. This includes identifying believers in Christ based on nationality, gender, ethnicity, skin colour, height, body structure, or social standing. However, fleshly identification is not how those in Christ are recognized or classified. Just as the Father sees us, we also ought to see each other. If we see someone of the kingdom of God after the flesh, then we are not seeing him or her from God's perspective. When you look at someone and you see gender rather than whom he or she is clothed with, your perspective is after the flesh. You are not identifying the person with Christ. You do not see Christ. In Christ, there is no gender (male or female). Gender has no bearing on how believers are identified in the body of Christ.

2 Corinthians 5:17 says in Christ, we are new creatures or a

new species of being. It means we are of a new kind or an unprecedented creation. This not only applies to the old man or the nature of sin being crucified with Christ (Romans 6:6-7) but also to our general classification. The old creature that was identified after the flesh no longer exists and we are now new creations in Christ. We have a nature that has no affiliation with gender, nationality, or social status. None of these things have any bearing on who we are now. Therefore, if we still function and identify people based on these things, then we do not see new creations, we are still seeing the old ones.

Furthermore, Galatians 3:28, by eliminating nationality, gender (male and female), and social status in the body of Christ, removes all the causes of divisions. According to the flesh, I am a citizen of the Bahamas and I have identification that supports that. However, being in Christ, my citizenship is in heaven and my earthly nationality or identity is irrelevant. Furthermore, by birth and in accordance with the flesh, I am identified as a male. However, in Christ, gender does not exist as I am neither male nor female. Moreover, based on the flesh, my wealth, social standing and even the color of my skin are fleshly identifiers. However, in Christ, none of these things define who I am. The message of the kingdom of God is that of unity and equality. Anything that would seek to foster divisions in the body of Christ must be abolished.

This is why Paul wholeheartedly says in Philippians 3:4-9:

4. Though I might also have confidence in the flesh. If any other man thinketh that he hath whereof he might trust in the flesh, I more:

5. Circumcised the eighth day, of the stock of Israel, of the tribe of Benjamin, an Hebrew of the Hebrews; as touching the law, a Pharisee;
6. Concerning zeal, persecuting the church; touching the righteousness which is in the law, blameless.
7. But what things were gain to me, those I counted loss for Christ.
8. Yea doubtless, and I count all things but loss for the excellency of the knowledge of Christ Jesus my Lord: for whom I have suffered the loss of all things, and do count them but dung, that I may win Christ,
9. And be found in him, not having mine own righteousness, which is of the law, but that which is through the faith of Christ, the righteousness which is of God by faith.

In using Paul's declaration as an example, whenever we place our confidence in the flesh or hold onto fleshly identification, then we are operating in our own righteousness, and this is not the righteousness of God.

Notice that Galatians 3:28 echoes the sentiment that has been the central theme of this book from the beginning, which is that we are all one in Christ. The definition of the word "one" is, "characterized by unity and being of the same quality." Being one or of the same quality means that everyone in Christ looks the same, has the same genetic makeup, and has the same standing. It is a statement of equality. We are people with no allegiance to earthy ethnicity, gender, or status. For in Christ, none of these qualities exist.

Notable Women in Scripture

Before concluding our discussion of women in ministry, I would be remiss not to mention several prominent women in Scripture who, despite the landscape of male dominance, became pioneering examples of the message of unity and equality. Particularly, we will look at Deborah in the Old Testament and Priscilla in the New Testament.

Deborah

To appreciate the significance of what the account of Deborah represents, there has to be an understanding of the setting in which she lived. During the time of Deborah, Israel was a patriarchal society under the rule of the Judges. The period of the Judges occurred between Israel's occupation of Canaan up to the time of Saul's appointment as king of Israel. As there was no king during this time, the judges were essentially charged with military and civil responsibilities for the nation. Hence, it was a position of leadership. The recurring theme of the book of Judges is when Israel sinned against God, they were delivered into the hands of oppressors. Consequently, they cried unto the Lord and He raised up judges to deliver them (Judges 3:7-11, 12-15). Of all the individuals who served as judges of Israel, Deborah was the only female. This in itself is substantial, especially considering the environment and dispensation in which she lived.

4. And Deborah, a prophetess, the wife of Lapidoth, she judged Israel at that time.
5. And she dwelt under the palm tree of Deborah between Ramah and Bethel in mount Ephraim: and the children of Israel came up to her for judgment. (Judges 4:4-5)

Regardless of her gender, all Israel, including both men and women, came to her for judgment. She sat in the seat of judgment and determined justice for the people. Not only was Deborah a judge, but she was also a prophetess. This means she was appointed by God and spoke on His behalf. In fact, throughout both the Old and New Testament, the Scripture mentions several prophetesses such as Miriam, Huldah, and Anna. If the Lord used women as His spokespersons under the dispensation of Law, certainly the dispensation of grace does not seek to do the opposite. On the contrary, it provides an atmosphere for greater opportunity.

During the time of Deborah, the Israelites were being oppressed by Jabin, king of Canaan, and Sisera, the commander of his army. Therefore, Deborah in her capacity as judge of Israel, went to Barak who was the military commander of Israel. Apparently, the Lord had already given him instructions concerning the battle along with the assurance of victory, but he neglected to go. In fact, the Lord was very specific with him identifying the number of men to take, as well as providing him with the battleplan. However, due to his inaction, Deborah went to him and reminded him of what the Lord said. Nevertheless, Barak said to her, "If thou wilt go with me, then I will go: but if thou wilt not go with me, then I will not go." She responded and said, "I will surely go with thee."

In combination, his response is both in defiance of what the Lord said, as well as an acknowledgment of Deborah's strength and influence as a leader. Concerning the latter, the statement demonstrates a level of confidence in Deborah that is fitting for someone in a leadership position and who functions in God's favor. However, as a consequence, she also informed him that the victory would not be for his honor because the Lord would deliver Sisera into the hands of a woman.

Subsequently, they attacked Sisera and his army and, with the help of the Lord, defeated them. However, Sisera fled and sought refuge in the tent of a Hebrew woman named Jael. She took him in, gave him milk to drink, and covered him with a blanket. Nevertheless, while he slept, she took a hammer and drove a nail of the tent through his temple, killing him. Thus, the prophecy of Deborah was fulfilled concerning a woman killing Sisera. Furthermore, God subdued Jabin, king of the Canaanites, and Israel prevailed against them and defeated them.

In a male-dominated era, certainly the story of Deborah goes against the established cultural norms and traditions of the time. Despite this, what I find interesting is that there is no record of her being dismissed or ostracized by men. Rather, the opposite is true. Based on what the Lord had appointed her to do, her leadership role was fully embraced to the benefit of everyone.

Priscilla

Before discussing the specifics regarding Priscilla, it is necessary to first establish a context of who she was. In Acts Chapter 18, based on the command from the Emperor Claudius, all Jews had to depart from Rome. Therefore, Aquila and his wife, Priscilla, left and went to Corinth. It was there that Paul met them and having the same occupation as tentmakers, he stayed and worked with them. Paul was in Corinth for a period of eighteen months preaching the gospel, and during this time, he established the Corinthian church. Furthermore, when he went to Syria and Ephesus, he took Aquila and Priscilla with him.

When Paul got to Ephesus, he stayed a short time preaching in the synagogue, but he left them there. It was at Ephesus, Aquila and Priscilla heard Apollos teaching.

> 24. And a certain Jew named Apollos, born at Alexandria, an eloquent man, and mighty in the scriptures, came to Ephesus.
> 25. This man was instructed in the way of the Lord; and being fervent in the spirit, he spake and taught diligently the things of the Lord, knowing only the baptism of John.
> 26. And he began to speak boldly in the synagogue: whom when Aquila and Priscilla had heard, they took him unto them, and expounded unto him the way of God more perfectly.
> 27. And when he was disposed to pass into Achaia, the brethren wrote, exhorting the disciples to receive him: who, when he was come, helped them much which had believed through grace:
> 28. For he mightily convinced the Jews, and that publickly, shewing by the scriptures that Jesus was Christ. (Acts 18:24-28)

Despite his eloquence, command of the Scriptures, boldness, and fervency, Apollos still had a limited perspective on the things of God, for he only knew the baptism of John. Apollos' knowledge was confined to the message that John the Baptist preached. The core message of John was repentance and water baptism (Matthew 3:1-12). As the forerunner of Christ, he said, "I indeed baptize you with water unto repentance: but He that cometh after me is mightier than I, whose shoes I am not worthy to bear: He shall baptize you with the Holy Ghost, and with fire" (Matthew 3:11). Therefore, despite being instructed in the way of the Lord, Apollos' knowledge of baptism was limited to that of water. He was unaware of the baptism of the Holy Spirit. This is similar to the experience Paul had in Ephesus in Acts 19:1-6. He found certain disciples and asked them if they had received the Holy Ghost since they believed. They responded and said, "We have not so much heard whether there be an Holy Ghost" (Acts 19:2), for they were baptized unto John's baptism.

Like Apollos, they also had a limited perspective on the things of God. Subsequently, Paul laid his hands on them, and they received the Holy Ghost. This adds to the point of the progressive nature of the New Testament that was made earlier. Despite the baptism of the Holy Spirit occurring on the Day of Pentecost in Acts Chapter 2, many were unaware of it.

Bear in mind that Aquila and Priscilla had been influenced by Paul's teaching for a year-and-a-half, and as fellow workers, they were instrumental in helping him establish the church at Corinth. They were both seasoned in the Word of God, which included knowledge of the baptism of the Holy Spirit and its impact. Therefore, when they heard Apollos speak, they realized that an important element was missing. Consequently, they took him unto them and expounded unto him the way of God more perfectly. Recognizing his leadership potential and that they were labourers together with God, they taught him concerning the baptism of the Holy Ghost. However, incorporated in this was the knowledge that Jesus was the Christ along with the fulness of the gospel message.

This was certainly a turning point in the ministry of Apollos and the Lord used both Aquila and Priscilla to influence him. As a result of Apollos' encounter with them, before he went to Corinth, the church at Ephesus gave him a letter of commendation for the Corinthian church to receive him. Based on the teaching they both imparted to him, he was now more knowledgeable concerning the things of God. Moreover, when he went to Corinth, he had a tremendous impact. Acts 18:28 says, "For he mightily convinced the Jews, showing by the Scriptures that Jesus was Christ." In fact, he was so instrumental that while addressing the divisions in the church at Corinth, Paul refers to his influence. He says in 1 Corinthians 3:6, "I have planted, Apollos watered; but God gives the increase." Despite the divisions that existed, this speaks of the significance of Apollos' teaching. Nevertheless, regarding the preferences of ministers, Paul makes it known to the Corinthian church that both he and Apollos were labourers together with God. With that said, the meeting with Aquila and Priscilla was extremely beneficial to Apollos and the Scripture bears witness to that.

As witnessed in Scripture, Aquila and Priscilla operated as a team in the spirit of unity. Furthermore, all the accounts when referring to their work use the personal pronoun "they," which means it directly refers to both of them. Priscilla was not quiet or on the sideline waiting to ask her husband at home. She also did not "learn in silence." Just like her husband, she taught the Scriptures and was instrumental in assisting Paul in his work, establishing the church, and assisting Apollos.

As mentioned in Chapter 4 of this book, Paul referred to both Aquila and Priscilla as helpers or fellowlabourers in Romans 16:3. This is an indication that both of them were involved with him in the preaching of the gospel. Also, recall that this is the same attribution he made concerning Apollos in 1 Corinthians 3:9. Additionally, he salutes them again in 2 Timothy 4:19. Finally, in his first letter to the Corinthians, Paul acknowledges that Aquila and Priscilla had a church in their house (1 Corinthians 16:19).

Based on what we have discussed, as a woman, Priscilla is a model in two regards. First, she is an example of a married woman working in tandem with her husband in the service of the Lord in the spirit of unity and equality. Additionally, she is also a testament for women in general. The references concerning her do not indicate that she was restricted based on her gender or that she was ignorant or unlearned in the Scriptures.

The limitations that religion and denominational doctrines impose on women in ministry are nonexistent in the example of Priscilla. Consider the fact that Priscilla, while at Corinth, was affiliated with the Corinthian church. As a companion of Paul and a fellow worker, she laboured with him at Corinth. Therefore, is it logical to think that he would say to the Corinthian church, "Let your women keep silence in the churches: for it is not permitted unto them to speak; but they are commanded to be under obedience, as also saith the Law. And if they will learn anything, let them ask their husbands at home: for it is a shame for women to speak in the church"? Of course not! Why would he salute her as a fellowlabourer and then advocate that other women be silent? Furthermore, he also left Aquila and Priscilla at Ephesus to whom the epistles to Timothy are addressed. Having assigned both of them there to preach the gospel, would it be practical to say, "But I suffer not a woman to teach, nor to usurp authority over the man, but to be in silence"? While I appeal to your intelligence, even in this it should be obvious that, in both instances, the scriptures are being misinterpreted.

Certainly, our discussion of notable women in the Bible who effectively functioned in the things of God is not limited to Deborah and Priscilla. Undoubtedly, more women can be added to the list. However, they serve as prime examples of women who operated in God's purpose, irrespective of their gender, resulting in tremendous accomplishments.

In Christ, there is unity and equality; identification based on gender or any other fleshly condition does not exist. If we can truly embrace this truth, then we can eliminate many of the divisions that exist in the body of Christ. Hence, the result would be a unified body dedicated to fulfilling the purpose of the Father. Just as Ephesians Chapter 2 speaks of removing walls, thereby fostering an atmosphere of unity and peace based on the truth of Scripture, let us remove the walls that make distinctions based on gender or any other attributes of the flesh.

At the conclusion of Chapter 2, several questions were presented relative to the function of women in ministry. It was the purpose of this book to address these questions by offering the true perspective of Scripture, based on the proper context of

Scripture. This provided an objective standard of truth as opposed to one based on personal feelings, denominational posture, and conjecture regarding the subject of women in ministry. Moreover, by addressing these questions, I hope that the body of Christ particularly women, truly experience the freedom that Scripture offers.

CONCLUSION

According to the *Free Dictionary* by Farlex, the word "freedom" means, "not restrained, obstructed or impeded." It is the ability to act without interference or confinement. While these definitions offer a generic insight concerning freedom, I submit that the true essence of the word is more associated with unity and equality. For when these two components are present, then true freedom can be realized.

Based on the content of this book, it should be abundantly clear that Scripture does not prohibit women from speaking in the church or place limitations on them regarding ministry even in a leadership role. The restrictions exist because of a misunderstanding of Scripture imposed by the religious establishment. This is the message of division, whereas the message of the kingdom of God is that of unity and equality. For in the kingdom of God, gender-bias does not exist. We are all clothed in Christ.

It is truly my hope that the content of this book would accomplish several objectives. First, as it pertains to women, I am optimistic that it will provide freedom for those who have been restrained from functioning in what the Father has purposed for you. This also includes those who have imposed limitations on themselves based on a misunderstanding of Scripture. Additionally, that it would confirm what you have always known deep inside, and you will make full proof of the gifts in you. Finally, may it serve as a shield against those who are otherwise persuaded.

To men, my plea is that you embrace this truth and come to the realization that a divided house cannot stand and that men and women are fellow labourers together with God. Recall that truth always leaves you in a better place. It does not deprive. Therefore, the acknowledgement that a woman can be a minister does not take away from a man. On the contrary, we all gain because we then benefit from that which every joint supplies. Unity and equality result in an indivisible house. Let us walk in freedom!

REFERENCES

- The Bahamas Constitution, 1973 Chapter 1, The Constitution is the supreme law. Retrieved January 12, 2018 from https://www.oas.org/juridico/mla/en/bhs/en_bhs-int-text-const.pdf
- AMG Publishers, The Hebrew-Greek Key Study Bible. Editor, Zodhiates, S. © 1995.
- Brethren [Def.] Strong's Concordance with Hebrew and Greek Lexicon Retrieved November 10, 2020 from https://www.blueletterbible.org/lang/Lexicon/Lexicon.cfm?strongs=G80&t=KJV
- Dominion [Def.] Strong's Concordance with Hebrew and Greek Lexicon Retrieved January 13, 2018 from https://www.blueletterbible.org/lang/Lexicon/Lexicon.cfm?strongs=H7287&t=KJV
- Dominion [Def.] Free Dictionary by Farlex Online. In the Free Dictionary by Farlex Retrieved January 19 2018, from http://www.thefreedictionary.com/dominion
- Man [Def.] Strong's Concordance with Hebrew and Greek Lexicon Retrieved January 17, 2018 from https://www.blueletterbible.org/lang/Lexicon/Lexicon.cfm?strongs=H120&t=KJV
- Alone [Def.] Free Dictionary by Farlex Online. In the Free Dictionary by Farlex Retrieved January 19 2018, from https://www.thefreedictionary.com/alone

- Help meet [Def.] Strong's Concordance with Hebrew and Greek Lexicon Retrieved March 20, 2019 from https://www.blueletterbible.org/lang/Lexicon/Lexicon.cfm?strongs=H5828&t=KJV
- Malmin, Ken and Kevin J. Conner, © 1983, Context of Scripture, A Textbook on How to Interpret the Bible Interpreting the Scriptures.
- Butler, Clement C, ©2017 God's Eternal Purpose Volume 1: The Establishment of God's Kingdom.
- Kennedy, John F., A rising tide lifts all boats.
- The Amplified Bible © 1993 by Zondervan.
- Lincoln, Abraham © 1858 A Divided House.
- Cleare, Dr. Betty, © 1994 Rightly Dividing the Word, Perspective of Scripture, New Life Christian Centre.
- Cleare, Dr. Betty, © 1994 Rightly Dividing the Word, Context of Scripture, New Life Christian Centre.
- Hairabedian, David, C., Published on July 31, 2011. Understanding the Four Spiritual Gifts. The Word of Knowledge and the Word of Wisdom.
- Butler, Clement C, © 2015 The Volume of the Book: Insights into Rightly Dividing the Word of Truth.
- Strong, James © 2009 Strong's Exhaustive Concordance of the Bible.
- Prophecy [Def.] Strong's Concordance with Hebrew and Greek Lexicon Retrieved November 1, 2020 from https://www.blueletterbible.org/lang/Lexicon/Lexicon.cfm?strongs=G4394&t=KJV
- Prophesying [Def.] Strong's Concordance with Hebrew and Greek Lexicon Retrieved November 1, 2020 from https://www.blueletterbible.org/lang/Lexicon/Lexicon.cfm?strongs=G4395&t=KJV
- Woman [Def.] Strong's Concordance with Hebrew and Greek Lexicon Retrieved January 20, 2018 from https://www.blueletterbible.org/lang/Lexicon/Lexicon.cfm?strongs=G1135&t=KJV
- Man [Def.] Strong's Concordance with Hebrew and Greek Lexicon Retrieved January 20 2018 from https://www.blueletterbible.org/

lang/Lexicon/Lexicon.cfm?strongs=G435&t=KJVOrdinances [Def.] Strong's Concordance with Hebrew and Greek Lexicon Retrieved January 22, 2018 from https://www.blueletterbible.org/lang/Lexicon/Lexicon.cfm?strongs=G3862&t=KJV

- Helpers [Def.] Strong's Concordance with Hebrew and Greek Lexicon Retrieved November 15, 2020 from https://www.blueletterbible.org/lang/Lexicon/Lexicon.cfm?strongs=G4904&t=KJV
- Deacon [Def.] Strong's Concordance with Hebrew and Greek Lexicon Retrieved November 15, 2020 from https://www.blueletterbible.org/lang/Lexicon/Lexicon.cfm?strongs=G1249&t=KJV
- Anthropology [Def.] Free Dictionary by Farlex Online. In the Free Dictionary by Farlex Retrieved January 19 2018, from http://www.thefreedictionary.com/anthropology
- Anthropology [Def.] Merriam-Webster Online. In Merriam-Webster. Retrieved January 20, 2018, from http://www.merriam-webster.com/dictionary/anthropology
- One [Def.] Free Dictionary by Farlex Online. In the Free Dictionary by Farlex Retrieved January 19 2018, from http://www.thefreedictionary.com/one
- Head [Def.] Strong's Concordance with Hebrew and Greek Lexicon Retrieved January 20 2018 from https://www.blueletterbible.org/lang/Lexicon/Lexicon.cfm?strongs=G2776&t=KJV
- Freedom [Def.]. Free Dictionary by Farlex Online. In the Free Dictionary by Farlex Retrieved January 25, 2018, from http://www.thefreedictionary.com/freedom
- Booth, Dawn, photographer, "Armor of God" [Contenders for the Faith]. Photograph. 2010. Retrieved December 9, 2020 from https://www.google.com/search?rlz=1C1CHBF_enBS731BS752&source=univ&tbm=isch&q=dawn+booth+photo+of+the+whole+armor+of+God&sa=X&ved=2ahUKEwi7yvq-gsTtAhXkAp0JHVPXCNUQjJkEegQIBRAB&biw=1536&bih=755#imgrc=jul37HAxzbtFjM.

www.ingramcontent.com/pod-product-compliance
Lightning Source LLC
Chambersburg PA
CBHW070456090426
42735CB00012B/2580